Divine Money

MUSLIM PHILANTHROPY AND CIVIL SOCIETY

Shariq Siddiqui

Divine Money

Islam, Zakat, and Giving in Palestine

Emanuel Schaeublin

INDIANA UNIVERSITY PRESS

This book is a publication of

Indiana University Press
Office of Scholarly Publishing
Herman B Wells Library 350
1320 East 10th Street
Bloomington, Indiana 47405 USA

iupress.org

© 2023 by Emanuel Schaeublin

All rights reserved
No part of this book may be reproduced or utilized in any form or by any means, electronic or mechanical, including photocopying and recording, or by any information storage and retrieval system, without permission in writing from the publisher. The paper used in this publication meets the minimum requirements of the American National Standard for Information Sciences—Permanence of Paper for Printed Library Materials, ANSI Z39.48-1992.

Manufactured in the United States of America

First printing 2023

Cover Design: Anne-Sophie Fraser

Library of Congress Cataloging-in-Publication Data

Names: Schaeublin, Emanuel, [date] author.
Title: Divine money : Islam, zakat, and giving in Palestine / Emanuel Schaeublin.
Description: Bloomington, Indiana : Indiana University Press, 2023. | Includes bibliographical references and index. |
Identifiers: LCCN 2023014482 (print) | LCCN 2023014483 (ebook) | ISBN 9780253066565 (cloth) | ISBN 9780253066572 (paperback) | ISBN 9780253066589 (adobe pdf)
Subjects: LCSH: Zakat—West Bank—Nablus. | Islamic giving. | Wealth—Moral and ethical aspects—West Bank—Nablus. | Public welfare—Religious aspects—Islam. | BISAC: SOCIAL SCIENCE / Islamic Studies | SOCIAL SCIENCE / Philanthropy & Charity
Classification: LCC BP180 .S33 2023 (print) | LCC BP180 (ebook) | DDC 297.5/4—dc23/eng/20230404
LC record available at https://lccn.loc.gov/2023014482
LC ebook record available at https://lccn.loc.gov/2023014483

CONTENTS

Acknowledgments vii

Note on Transliteration, Translation, and Anonymization xi

Introduction: *An Anthropological Perspective on Zakat* 1

1. Fieldwork under Military Rule: *Subjecting Oneself to Lateral Disciplining* 22
2. Zakat Institutions on Shifting Grounds 41
3. Concealing and Exposing Need: *Shyness, Piety, and Dignity* 59
4. The Piety of Giving: *Modeling Direct Zakat Interactions* 75
5. The Ethics of Giving and Market Transactions 92
6. The Other World and the Occupation 112

Notes 133

References 145

Index 159

ACKNOWLEDGMENTS

Myriad gestures of giving sustained the production of this book. A variety of people devoted their attention to support my fieldwork, reflect on findings, and put thoughts on paper. "Attention is the rarest and purest form of generosity," as Simone Weil beautifully put it, and without all the great people generously devoting their attention to the work of others, science could not flourish.

A wide range of people made ethnographic fieldwork from 2013 to 2014 in the city of Nablus possible by teaching me how to conduct myself respectfully in various kinds of interactions and tactfully research the multilayered sensitivities at play in giving without intruding into people's lives. I am particularly grateful to my research assistant Marah Az, whom I introduce in the first chapter. Her ethnographic observations of the zakat practices between women are an important element in the argument developed in this book. The people at the Hammouz Café in Nablus offered me the comfort of a second home with their generosity and their sense of humor. They provided refreshment on hot days and the warmth of a wood stove during the heavy snowfall in December 2013. In Nablus and across the West Bank and Jerusalem, many good people looked after me and let me become part of their lives. Out of respect for their privacy under the difficult conditions of military occupation, I refrain from mentioning their names here. Visiting me in Nablus, Jonas Opperskalski and Iwan Schauwecker took photographs, several of which illustrate this book.

Regarding institutional aspects, my fieldwork is indebted to the Ministry of Awqaf of the Palestinian Authority, the former mayor of Nablus Adly Yaish, the Nablus Zakat Committee and its employees, the municipal library of Nablus, and the Institut Français du Proche-Orient in Jerusalem, who hosted me as an associated researcher. Moreover, historians and archivists at the municipal library, various scholars at Najah University, and various former members of the Nablus Zakat Committee sat down to have long conversations with me about the past and present of zakat practice in Palestine. Fahmi Ansari, in his beautiful library in East Jerusalem, kindly shared his thoughts on the history of zakat practices in nineteenth-century Palestine on several occasions.

With a view to the research process, I am deeply grateful to Morgan Clarke at the University of Oxford, who introduced me to anthropology and provided a perfect combination of orientation and freedom as a doctoral supervisor. His generous reactions to countless drafts and his sense of humor turned the research project that led to this book into a both transformative and highly enjoyable experience. At the Institute of Social and Cultural Anthropology in Oxford, I am particularly indebted to the advice of Paul Dresch, Ramon Sarró, and Mohammed Taleb, as well as to Seohyung Kim, Chihab El Khachab, Susan MacDougall, Azim Islam, and Alexander Donnelly for many animated conversations. My time at Oxford and in Nablus would not have been possible without the generous support of the Berrow Foundation at Lincoln College and of the Swiss National Science Foundation.

Jonathan Benthall at University College London first encouraged me to conduct research on zakat in 2008 and continued to support me ever since. We exchanged thoughts on walks in various countries and commented on one another's writings. From 2010 to 2011, I spent one year at the Institut Français du Proche-Orient in Damascus benefiting from the extensive knowledge of Youssef Salameh, Hassan Abbas, Maher Sharif, and many others. The University of Birzeit in the West Bank hosted me as an exchange student in 2004–2005. At Birzeit, I attended my first anthropology seminar, which Ismail Nashif was teaching in Arabic. The seminar involved participant observation exercises during cultural events organized by European organizations in Ramallah. At the University of Geneva, Marguerite Gavillet-Matar, Alain de Libera, Maroun Aouad, the late Abdelwahab Meddeb, and others provided excellent introductions to Arabic and Arab philosophy.

The arguments developed in this book benefited from discussions about my findings on zakat in various scholarly settings, including the 2019 conference of the Society of Palestinian Anthropologists, or "Insaniyyat," on the overarching theme of "Thinking without the State" in the anthropology of Palestine; an excellent panel "Institutional Surveillance and the Ethics of Observation" convened by the late Sonja Luehrmann at the 2018 AAA conference in San Francisco; the departmental seminar in social anthropology at the University of Manchester convened by Michelle Obeid, where I received particularly extensive feedback from Pnina Werbner; and the 2022 workshop "Reckoning with God: Divine-Human Relations after the Arab Spring" convened by Joud Al Korani. In Palestine, I had more helpful exchanges of ideas discussing my research at the Institut Français du Proche-Orient in Jerusalem and the University of Birzeit, as well as the University of al-Azhar and the Islamic University, both located in Gaza City.

Among many other things in life, my friend Ibrahim Jamal taught me the art of effectively dropping colloquial Arabic expressions in specific moments and situational circumstances. Monika Bolliger hosted me various times in her foreign correspondent apartment in East Jerusalem. I am very grateful to her for all the conversations and exchanges over the years. Several ideas about the link between face-to-face interactions and collectively held assumptions about the world as developed in this book have also been taken up in film productions. I advised my brother Cyril Schäublin on using anthropological ideas and ethnographic methods in the development of screenplays and the production of two films set in Switzerland: *Those Who Are Fine* (2017) and *Unrest* (2022).

The writing of the manuscript and its navigation through peer review have been supported by grants from the University of Zurich and the Swiss Federal Institute of Technology, ETH Zurich, and the Swiss Academy of Social Sciences and Humanities 2020 gold award for the best research paper. Anne-Sophie Fraser designed the diagrams and the cover of the book. For various comments on drafts, I thank the anonymous reviewers at Indiana University Press, Jaida Samudra, Samuli Schielke, Michael Feener, Shariq Siddiqui, Monika Bolliger, Jonas Röllin, Florian Leu, Johannes Quack, Nicole Egloff, Jonathan Benthall, Cyril Schäublin, and Dominik Müller. For various acts of care and conversations, I thank Greta Korthals, Othmar Schäublin, Qais Kasabri, Yassir Abdel-Hafez, Anne-Sophie Fraser, Michael Blaser, Michelle Lebaron, Maged Senbel, Dilyara Müller, Adina Rom, Simon Mason, Mae Chokr, Ramy al-Asheq, Dominik Gross, Benoît Challand, Nura Khalili, Mohammed Dahmani, Haythem Bastawi, Nada Abdulla, Pat Brown, Farea Muslimi, Maysaa Shujaa Al-Din, Adrian Brändli, and the late Victor Kocher. I dedicate this book to Eleonora, Nathaniel, and most of all Victoria, whose love and stubbornness has widened my soul.

None of the people or institutions mentioned here are accountable for any mistake in this book, and I bear the sole responsibility for the thoughts and observations expressed in it.

NOTE ON TRANSLITERATION, TRANSLATION, AND ANONYMIZATION

I follow the Latin transliteration of Arabic words as defined by the *International Journal for Middle Eastern Studies* (IJMES), with the exception of Arabic words commonly used in English, such as mufti, Quran, sadaqa, sheikh, and zakat. For translating longer verses from the Quran, I rely on the translation of Muhammad Asad (1980). Throughout the book, I consistently write God rather than Allah (even in citations). All interlocutors' names are pseudonyms with the exception of publicly known personalities. I have altered incidental details of people's lives to protect their identities. Throughout the research undertaken for this book, I sought to comply with the *Ethical Guidelines for Good Research Practice* provided by the Association of Social Anthropologists of the United Kingdom and the Commonwealth.

Glossary

ajr	account of good deeds, recompense
ḥadīth	sayings and deeds ascribed to the Prophet or to people from his entourage
ḥaqq	rightful share of wealth to which those in need are entitled
'ibāda	worship of God
maskīn	helpless, one of the categories eligible to receive zakat
mu'āmalāt	social interactions and transactions
rizq	divine material provision, sustenance, legitimate profit from trade
sadaqa	supererogatory alms
tawakkul	reliance on God
thawāb	divine recompense in the Hereafter
waqf	endowment of immovable property
zakat	obligatory alms

Divine Money

Introduction

An Anthropological Perspective on Zakat

In Palestinian neighborhoods where the Islamic tradition shapes public life, a seemingly mundane gift of money or food to a person in need can invoke the presence of God. People explain the presence of God in the act of giving in two complementary ways. First, the goods or money given really belongs to God (not the giver) and is therefore an expression of His generosity. Second, the gift counts toward a system of divine bookkeeping from which God will reward the giver either in this life or in the Hereafter. Giving is an important part of practicing Islam. Indeed, the annual donation of zakat, meaning a share of one's liquid assets, is one of the pillars of Islam. The Quran obliges well-off Muslims—specifically those whose annually held financial and material assets are worth at least the equivalent of eighty-five grams of gold—to give away 2.5 percent of their movable wealth in the form of money, food, or material goods to people in need each year.[1] Such zakat is usually given during the month of Ramadan, but it can also be distributed along with supererogatory gifts known as sadaqa throughout the year. The obligation to provide zakat has given rise to direct but informal zakat transactions between individuals within neighborhoods and formal institutions that collect and distribute zakat to households in need of support.

This book presents an anthropological perspective on Islamic giving in the West Bank, one of the Palestinian territories occupied by Israel since 1967.[2] While zakat is not part of the formal taxation system of the West Bank, zakat institutions and direct zakat giving play an important role in providing welfare to households in financial distress. Based on my ethnographic fieldwork in the city of Nablus, I analyze how zakat institutions function in the social and political context of contemporary Palestine and explore how people reference Islamic scripture to negotiate the social tensions that arise around differences of wealth. In the absence of a reliable public safety net, many of my interlocutors interpret acts of giving as an expression of God's generosity and His infinite ability to provide for humans. Such invocations of the divine in apparently mundane interactions open up possibilities to live good and ethical Muslim lives even during times of political repression and economic stagnation.

Divine Zakat, Tactful Giving, and the Problem of Shame

Because the recipients of charity cannot usually reciprocate, gifts always have the potential to wound them (Mauss [1925] 2016, 177). Being given zakat tends be felt as *'ayb* (shameful) because it potentially marks the recipients and sometimes their extended families as inferior, needy, or dependent. Avoiding this wounding effect requires tact and discretion on behalf of both the giver and receiver of zakat. It often involves gestures aimed at obscuring and depersonalizing the origin of the gift, thereby enabling the givers to constitute themselves as mere channels of God's generosity. By effacing their own role in the circulation of God's material provisions, givers display modesty and appear to be shaping themselves into "a medium for God's will" (Mittermaier 2019, 140). In this context, zakat can take on the status of divine money—something that is assumed to belong to God, not the giver. Enacting gifts to people in need as transfers of divine money mitigates their potential to bring shame to receivers.

The practice of zakat in Nablus is about maintaining a balance in relationships between people in very different financial situations. Giving zakat is supposed to cleanse the community of negative feelings while morally purifying the wealth of the giver. Indeed, the associated verb *zakkī*, as used in the Quran, means "to purify oneself," for example by giving part of one's wealth away. Receiving zakat is widely considered the "right" (*ḥaqq*) of those in need. The Arabic word *ḥaqq* also means the "rightful measure," as when two parties in a transaction negotiate for their fair share or a seller sets a "just price" for a good offered for sale. Individuals involved in every transaction are expected to render to the other party their "rightful share" (*ḥaqq*), lest God deduct points from His accounting of their good deeds.

Although essential to being a good Muslim, giving zakat requires tact between affluent people and those who are out of money. Tactful interactions across differences of wealth depend on the "embodiment" (Mahmood 2005) and "mutual display" (Schaeublin 2019) of Muslim piety (*taqwā*), which subsumes a number of virtues, such as modesty, patience, reliance on God, and gratitude. While this is especially pronounced in face-to-face interactions between givers and receivers of zakat, Muslims are encouraged to display such virtues in all social interactions. Thus, Muslims constantly negotiate ethical conundrums such as "How should one act?" "What kind of person does one want to be?" and "What makes a good life in community with others?" throughout their interactions with others. Examining such ethical negotiations in the context of zakat giving is the focus of this book.

Anthropology of Ethical Interaction and the Islamic Tradition of Giving

Many anthropologists have studied how people reflect on and pragmatically respond to such ethical questions in different social and historical contexts. Michel Foucault's (1986, 1997) work on the "care of the self" or "technologies of the self" has been particularly influential in the examination of why and how people cultivate certain virtues or qualities over others (Laidlaw 2014). Giving is not only about cultivating oneself, however. It essentially concerns how one relates to and interacts with others. In this context, Erving Goffman's (1959) theory on self-presentation is also useful. In presenting themselves to "Others," people seek to display certain virtues or qualities to prove that they are "good" persons. In a recent book proposing an anthropology of ethics starting from the study of interactions, Webb Keane (2015) draws on Goffman to examine how ethical questions permeate people's everyday lives. Keane views self-presentation as a kind of "ethical work on the self" (2015, 147) rather than as a superficial or cynical performance (MacIntyre [1981] 2007, 116). He argues that people seek to establish their "ethical worth in the eyes, or ears, of others" and give "an account" of themselves throughout their everyday interactions (Keane 2015, 138).

This perspective is particularly suitable for studying the connections among ethics, wealth, and the Islamic tradition. The Quran (93, 10) explicitly acknowledges that the obligation to give arises from relations with others when it reminds people that "the one who asks [for help] is not to be turned away." For centuries, good ethical conduct in Muslim communities has been inherently tied to how people spend their wealth, since they have a duty to care for other people in their immediate proximity and surrounding areas (Hallaq 2009, 296). In Muslim communities, how a person spends their wealth is thus subject to public observation and ethical judgment. Leaving need uncovered, as it were, by failing to give to others their rightful share taints the reputations of wealthy people and casts doubt on whether they are good Muslims. People thus reinforce the social obligation to give throughout their interactions with others in the community.

This book further builds on the anthropology of ethics by examining how Muslim Palestinians invoke a divine presence in their everyday expressions and gestures when they are interacting with others.[3] It explores how their references to Islamic texts constitute their social interactions as a field of ethical practice and moral judgment.[4] Talal Asad (1986, 1993, 2003) suggests that it is useful to study Islam as a discursive tradition—that is, as a continuous and socially embodied argument that draws on Islamic texts such as the Quran and Prophetic traditions to answer ethical questions concerning how to live as a good person. The presence of Islamic references in everyday speech comes into view as discourse in face-to-face interaction (Hacking 2004).[5] In other words, Islamic concepts and scriptures shape how people present themselves to one another in social interactions (Goffman 1959). While this phenomenon is not limited to Islam, the duty to observe, judge, and interfere in the ethical conduct of neighbors has led to particularly explicit discussions among Islamic scholars across the centuries (Cook 2001). Note also that Christian communities used to make frequent references to God in everyday interactions; these now survive as vestiges in expressions such as *goodbye* ("God be with you") in English or *adieu* ("I commend you to God") in French.

The anthropology of ethics helps decenter debates on Islam and move beyond the "cultural exceptionalism" that all too often has characterized analyses of Islam and the Middle East by non-Muslims (Schielke 2015, 13–14). Rather than singling out Islam as a religion informed by certain beliefs in transcendental realities, the anthropology of ethics allows for studying how Muslims address ethical questions (and paradoxes) in practice.[6] Building on this perspective, the ethnographic study of zakat provided in this book brings Islam into view as an ethical tradition unfolding in lived practice rather than as a religion centered on what people believe.[7] Consequently, the anthropological perspective adopted in this book focuses on how people invoke God to shape their interactions with one another (see also Schielke 2019). As an anthropologist, I am concerned with how ideas about God, the Hereafter, or an invisible world arise from social interactions and are given a presence in this world (Mittermaier 2013; see also T. Asad 2020 and Rahman 2022), where they have tangible repercussions—for instance, by allowing people to declare that gifts of zakat are God's money.

I approach the Islamic tradition as a "societal" discourse wherein "all kinds of institutions find simultaneous expression: religious, legal, moral, economic and political" (Messick 1993, 5; in reference to Mauss [1925] 2016, 58). The study of ethical interaction unsettles distinctions between religious and economic spheres of life. Furthermore, ethical self-presentations in interactions with others can have political implications. The anthropologist Saba Mahmood (2005, 4) has written about Muslim women in Cairo who cultivate gestures of shyness in public social interactions to cultivate piety simultaneously as an "inward ... disposition and ... practical conduct." Commenting on this research, Salwa Ismail (2007) notes that such public displays of Muslim piety in social interactions are "political" because they have a disciplinary effect on others. In this book, I introduce the term *lateral disciplining* to analyze such disciplinary effects of everyday interactions on the basis of ethnography from the Palestinian West Bank. Such disciplining is "lateral" because it is not carried out from an established position of authority. Through the display of virtue in their interactions, people pressure one another as equals to behave morally, including by distributing a portion of their wealth throughout the community.

Such social interactions are not stable, however. They generate tension and are subject to continued discussion by Islamic scholars (Cook 2001). Traditional interpretations of Islamic texts distinguish acts of worship (*'ibāda*) such as prayer and fasting from social interactions and transactions (*mu'āmalāt*).[8] Muslim piety is thus only partly constituted through worship and the individual care of the self. In many writings by historical Islamic scholars, the sections on how to interact appropriately vastly exceed the sections on worship (Anderson 2011, 4). Consequently, historical Islamic scholars conceived of ethics as "a quality and function of social exchange" rather than as a Foucauldian process of self-cultivation (4). Like other traditions based on sacred texts, the Islamic tradition exhibits a certain "plasticity" (Clarke 2018, 3, 307) in adapting to changing political, economic, and social contexts. The practice of zakat is no exception.

Historicizing Zakat

In different societies throughout history, interpreters of the Quranic obligation to give zakat have pointed to its dual character (Hurgronje [1882] 1957; Hallaq 2009, 231; Fauzia 2013, 47). On the one hand, they define almsgiving as a virtue and key element in the worship of God. According to the Quran, all wealth originates from God and affluent Muslims are obliged to give part of it away lest their prayers become void. On the other hand, they ascribe an institutional character to zakat when intermediaries are involved in collecting financial donations from the wealthy and distributing them to those in need. The Quran (9, 60) allows for such intermediaries in the third clause of a key passage, often quoted by my interlocutors and in traditional scholarly texts, that lists eight categories of potential beneficiaries of zakat and sadaqa. Such funds can be distributed to (1) the poor, including orphans as a subcategory; (2) the needy or helpless; (3) those who are in charge of collecting and distributing zakat; (4) those whose hearts are to be won over; (5) the freeing of human beings from bondage; (6) those who are overburdened with debts; (7) support for every struggle "in God's cause"; and (8) the wayfarer.[9] Since the Quran permits zakat to be donated to individuals in need as well as to collectivities to support worthy causes, historic zakat practices have ranged from direct, face-to-face transactions between givers and receivers to taxes collected by various Islamic polities (Bashear 1993, 99–108; Scott 1987; Singer 2008, 47–48). As with the old English tithing system, rulers in certain historical contexts have referred to the religious obligation to give zakat as a justification for extracting taxes from populations under their control.

In the twentieth century, zakat became an integral aspect of an Islamic state envisioned by many political movements. In the context of capitalist or socialist concepts of a just society that were spreading throughout Muslim-majority countries in the twentieth century, a number of Muslim political thinkers started to envision zakat giving as an institutional mechanism for the redistribution of wealth in modern state structures (Tripp 2006). Islamic political thinkers such as the Egyptian Sayyid Qutb (2000) explicitly connected the notion of zakat to the idea of social justice.[10] In *Social Justice in Islam*, originally published in 1949, Qutb presents an argument that zakat as a modern legal right "should be imposed by a centralized disciplinary state run by a vanguard of enlightened believers" (Rech 2017, 166; for a critique of this project, see Hallaq 2014).

Where Islamic political forces have exercised state power, zakat has sometimes become part of the tax system. This is the case in Pakistan, Saudi Arabia (Derbal 2022, 80–81), Sudan, and, since 2011, the Gaza Strip of Palestine under the governance of the Islamic Hamas movement (Schaeublin 2014, 25).[11] Where Islamic political movements have remained in opposition to state authorities, they have often built nongovernmental structures for collecting and distributing zakat and sadaqa. Such nongovernmental zakat institutions flourished when state governments such as those in Egypt (Atia 2013; Tugal 2013) and India (Osella and Osella 2009) retreated from providing welfare in the 1970s. Around the same time, transnational zakat institutions became an increasingly important part of the global humanitarian system (Benthall and Bellion-Jourdan 2009; Petersen 2014).

A number of anthropologists have argued that the transformation in the global political economy changed how people understood Islamic giving. As capitalist ideologies spread to Muslim-majority countries, people increasingly saw giving zakat and sadaqa as an act of personal piety aimed at gaining spiritual merit. Anthropologists working in Egypt suspect that giving to the poor to gain points for good deeds only became a dominant way of thinking after the "logic of the market" started to engulf religious practice in the 1970s (Mittermaier 2013, 275, 286; see also Schielke 2015, 22). Retsikas (2014, 337) similarly observes that in Indonesia since the 1970s, zakat has been increasingly "reconceptualized as philanthropy" in a way that privileges the "transcendental character" of zakat as bringing forth reward in the Hereafter rather than as social duty. These anthropologists suggest that people started overemphasizing the celestial rewards of zakat because seeking personal salvation by accumulating good deeds resonated particularly well with an ethic of market capitalism rooted in personal merit and individual responsibility. (These observations are captured in the first model of zakat discussed below.)

Other perspectives on zakat practices since the 1970s have focused more on the social duty to pass on to those in need whatever God has provided. Mittermaier (2019, 4) argues that the notion of justice underlies Islamic giving in Cairo, for example. Meanwhile, a recent ethnography on rural Bosnia emphasizes that Islamic giving practices are expressions of divine generosity (Henig 2019). Such readings sustain an understanding of "Muslim life" as "an ongoing exchange of blessing, prosperity and fortune, for good deeds, merits and prayers between the living, the dead and the Almighty . . . a perpetual flow or 'vital exchange' of divine grace and abundance" (Henig 2019, 225). The idea of zakat as a divine obligation indeed challenges economic discourses of individual responsibility and casts doubt on whether the "calculative logic of the market" really does fully determine contemporary practices of Islamic giving. (This argument is implied in the second model of zakat discussed below.)

Gift Theory and Zakat: Two Models

In his famous essay *The Gift*, anthropologist Marcel Mauss ([1925] 2016, 81–84) describes alms as a sacrifice to God, the value of which is redirected to the poor. God then compensates the giver in the form of spiritual merit. Gifts of alms therefore always involve a triad: a receiver, a giver, and God (or some other entity that registers spiritual merit). Zakat giving involves such a triad in that it is "oriented toward the Other in need [receiver], the self [giver], and God, all at once" (Mittermaier 2014, 527; see also Falcioni 2012, 446). The triad of receiver, giver, and God emerges in the Islamic textual tradition and in the everyday social interactions between givers and receivers invoking God's blessings (Schielke 2019, 3).

There are two ways of conceptualizing the relationships among the three members of the zakat triad and thinking about the divine presence in economic transactions of giving. One builds on Mauss's concept of "spiritual merit" and Kochyut's (2009, 109–110) application of this idea to the Islamic tradition, wherein God recompenses generous Muslims in the Hereafter. The second model represents the idea that God is present in zakat transactions because all wealth originates from Him. With the assistance of graphic designer Anne-Sophie Fraser, I have developed diagrams for these two models for thinking about the presence of the divine in zakat interactions.

The first model of zakat is one of circular exchange (fig. 0.1). It emerges from the idea that gifts of zakat are registered by God as good deeds in a divine account. From this credit of good deeds, God will recompense the giver either in this life in the form of blessings or in the Hereafter by raising the person's position in paradise. A passage of the Quran (64, 17) discussing gifts to the people in need makes this idea explicit: "If you offer up to God a goodly loan [*qarḍ*], He will amply repay you for it." This way of arranging things orients zakat relationships primarily toward the Hereafter and characterizes zakat as a "gift to God" (Mittermaier 2019). This model corresponds directly to Mauss's theory of almsgiving, wherein accruing spiritual merit raises the status of the giver in the Hereafter to sustain a "triadic reciprocity" among receivers, givers, and God (Kochyut 2009).

A problem for this understanding of God's presence in zakat transactions is that the Quran (24, 38) explicitly states that God's provisions cannot be accounted for, since "God grants sustenance unto whom He wills, beyond all reckoning." The next model addresses this conundrum.

The second model of zakat (fig. 0.2) builds on the traditional image of God as the origin of all material goods, the "sole and ultimate Owner ... of everything, including human beings and all they possess" (Hallaq 2009, 296). His provisions reach people at different levels of intensity, however: God provides an abundance of material goods to the wealthy. The wealthy are obliged (both to God and to others) to pass on some of their material wealth to those who are not as well-provisioned by God. The latter receive less directly from God, but these gifts are supplemented by zakat. Zakat is the rightful share (*ḥaqq*) of God's provisions to which people in need are entitled (Quran 17, 26; 51, 19; 70, 24–25).

This model of zakat focuses more on the circulation of material goods during people's lifetimes than on the Hereafter. Here, the obligation of zakat giving is aimed at "preventing the resources required to meet the daily needs of life from being hogged by the rich"; the central problem addressed in this context is "not inequality but rather what one *does* from one's position within a given hierarchy" (Mittermaier 2019, 183; original emphasis). The Islamic scriptures make

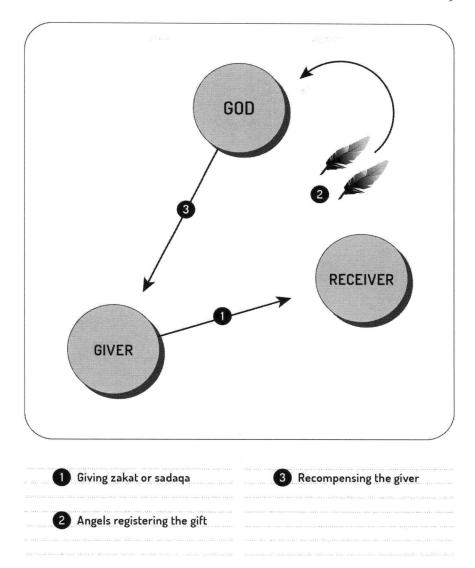

- **1** Giving zakat or sadaqa
- **2** Angels registering the gift
- **3** Recompensing the giver

Figure 0.1. Model 1: Zakat as a loan to God. © Anne-Sophie Fraser

people aware that no one other than God sustains the ability to give (Dresch 1998, 114–115). All humans start out life as "poor receivers" of God's largesse. Against this background, zakat emerges as the obligation of those blessed with God's generosity to pass some of it on to the ones left out. If Muslims were to obey the obligation of zakat consistently, God's generosity would ceaselessly flow from its original human recipients to those whose provisions are blocked,

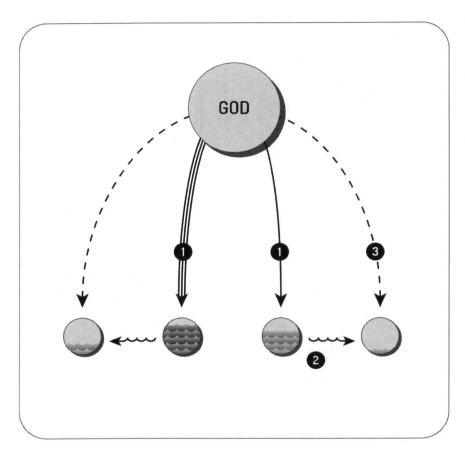

1. God's material provision
2. Recipients passing on some of their wealth to those struck by financial scarcity
3. God's material provision is blocked or delayed

Figure 0.2. Model 2: Zakat as passing on God's wealth. © Anne-Sophie Fraser

so that eventually everyone would be "covered" (*mastūr*) or "taken care of" (Elyachar 2005, 159). Ultimately, only God is rich, and wealthy people are mere "channels" of divine provision (Mittermaier 2019, 130, 135). Each of these two models represents a possible way of using Islamic discourse to address the apparent paradox between unequal levels of material security among people and their presumed moral equality before God.[12]

Between Social Compulsion and Technology of the Self

Through analysis of my study of transactions and gifts in the wider field of social interactions in Nablus, this book documents how zakat and sadaqa often align with the social compulsion to cover the needs of relatives and people in one's proximity to prevent shame. Drawing on Mauss ([1925] 2016), Dresch (1998, 116) argues that much giving springs from a "compulsion" that "does not reduce to rules or to forms of argument. The complexities of later jurisprudence on gifts and alms ... thus obscure the simplicity one sees in giving." Historically, explicit framings of generous gifts as zakat and sadaqa may only be part of this more general social compulsion to give, "for giving sadaqa was known and generosity to the poor a virtue before the [Islamic] revelation," as argued by Dresch (1998, 117). In the late nineteenth century, for example, nomadic tribes in the Arabian Peninsula ignorant of scriptural Islam framed generous giving as sadaqa. The traveler Charles Doughty describes their understanding of sadaqa as "the willing God's tribute and godly kindness of an upright man, spared out of his own necessity, to the relief of another" ([1888] 1936, 493; discussed in Benthall and Bellion-Jourdan 2009, 20).

The idea of divine bookkeeping takes up this compulsion to give and makes giving an integral part of the "technology of the self" of pious Muslims. According to Foucault (1997, 225), "technologies of the self ... permit individuals to effect by their own means, or with the help of others, a certain number of operations on their own bodies and souls, thoughts, conduct, and way of being, so as to transform themselves in order to attain a certain state of happiness, purity, wisdom, perfection, or immortality." Foucault roughly distinguishes such technologies among the ancient Greeks (taking care of the self as a constant "practice" of virtues), the Stoics (keeping an account of oneself, writing down what one did and analyzing the effects), and the early Christians (monitoring one's own thoughts and keeping them clean from sinful ones, excavating guilt, speaking the truth about one's sinful thoughts— or deeds—to someone else and thereby freeing or cleansing oneself from them). The idea of trading with God by gaining points for virtuous actions constitutes another type of technology of the self. It enables specific ways of making one's actions transparent to oneself and shapes the daily practices of Muslims (Schaeublin 2021).

By analyzing the tensions between social compulsion and technology of the self at play in giving in Nablus, this book explores how people balance social responsibility to others and personal piety. This sheds light on how people resist and react to the political economy of occupied Palestine at the micro level of their ethical lives (Keane 2015) by referring to the Islamic scriptures in their everyday interactions and giving zakat tactfully to avoid wounding the recipients. The next section provides background information for understanding zakat practices in the Palestinian context.

Historical and Political Context of Islamic Giving in Palestine

The region that is now contested as Israel or Palestine covers roughly thirty thousand square kilometers stretching eastward from the western shore of the Mediterranean Sea (including what came to be known as the Gaza Strip at the southern end of the coast) to the west bank of the Jordan River (an area subsequently known as the West Bank) and from the Lebanon border in the north to a narrow point at the Gulf of Aqaba in the southeast (fig. 0.3). A few square kilometers of flat, fertile land along the Mediterranean coast give way to dry hills covered with olive groves. These are the foothills of a high mountain range running north to south parallel to the coast. (The city of Jerusalem at the center is situated 800 meters above sea level.) East of the mountain range, the territory drops into the Jordan valley toward the city of Jericho and the Dead Sea (420 meters below sea level).

Although the exact political borders have been disputed many times, this is approximately the geography of the area known as Palestine that was part of the Ottoman Empire under the caliph in Istanbul until 1918, when the British Mandate of Palestine replaced Ottoman rule. (The caliphate as an institution ended in 1923.) After the British left Palestine in 1948, the new independent State of Israel claimed part of the Palestine region as its own (see the area marked as Israel in fig. 0.3). The West Bank, including the Palestinian cities of Jerusalem, Ramallah, Hebron, and Nablus, subsequently fell under the rule of the nascent Jordanian nation-state, while the Gaza Strip was administered by the Egyptian military. This political scenario changed again in 1967, when Israel began building settlements in the West Bank and the Gaza Strip (in addition to parts of Syria and Egypt). Significant portions of the Palestinian population were forcibly displaced by the State of Israel in 1948 and again in 1967, and the West Bank and Gaza Strip became known as "occupied Palestinian territories."

Figure 0.3. Map of Palestinian cities and governorates before Israeli occupation in 1967. © Graduate Institute Geneva

Political opposition to Israeli occupation of these Palestinian territories was mostly led by the Palestinian Liberation Organization (PLO), an umbrella for various political movements organizing themselves in exile under the leadership of Yassir Arafat's Fatah Movement. Then, in 1987, the Palestinian population began protesting the Israeli occupation; this popular uprising came to be known as the First Intifada. An offshoot of the Muslim Brotherhood in Palestine calling itself the Islamic Resistance Movement, or Hamas, joined the struggle against the occupation. Hamas did not join the PLO, however, and instead grew into the most important Islamist counterpart to Arafat's more secular nationalist Fatah Movement, which also uses religious vocabulary and symbolism in the struggle for national liberation.

The First Intifada led to official negotiations between Palestinian politicians representing the population in the territories and the government of Israel in the early 1990s. When these talks faltered, the Israeli government began negotiating secretly with PLO leaders who were living in exile, mostly in Tunis, at the time.[13] They signed an agreement in Oslo in 1993 (known as Oslo Accord I) to establish the Palestinian Authority (PA), which was expected to gradually develop into an independent and viable Palestinian state alongside the State of Israel. Until then, the PA would administer the West Bank and Gaza Strip under a form of Palestinian self-governance even as the territories remained under Israeli military occupation. Following this agreement, thousands of people who had been in exile with the PLO returned to Palestine. Most of them moved to what was then the small village of Ramallah and took up jobs in the newly created PA administration there. Israel did not allow the PA to establish itself in East Jerusalem because Palestinians claim that area as the capital of their nascent independent state. Ramallah was deemed a less contentious territory, so most of the institutions resulting from Palestinian state-building programs have been set up there. In the process, Ramallah has been transformed into a city.

The Oslo Accord of 1993 also sealed a deal between Palestinian Yassir Arafat's Fatah Movement and Israeli Yitzhak Rabin's secular Labor Party. Religious political forces on both sides opposed the agreement in part because they had been excluded from the negotiations (Zalzberg 2019), with Hamas constituting the greatest challenge to Fatah's domination of the PA. In light of the atrocious acts of violence committed by both Israelis and Palestinians who opposed concessions to the other side, the peace process sketched out in the Oslo agreement fell apart. A Second Intifada, lasting from 2000 to 2006, was met with violent suppression by Israeli armed forces. Israel also dismantled all Israeli settlements in the Gaza Strip in 2005. In the West Bank, however, new

Figure 0.4. View of Nablus from the southern mountain, Mount Gerizim. © Author

settlements have continued to be constructed from 1993 until the time of the writing of this book.

The City of Nablus

To study Islamic giving in Israeli-occupied Palestine, I spent a year from September 2013 to August 2014 conducting fieldwork in Nablus, an ancient city in the northern West Bank with about 120,000 residents (fig. 0.4). Situated in a valley between Mount Ebal to the north and Mount Gerizim to the south, Nablus is marked by the history of Palestine, starting with its succession of foreign rulers of the Ottoman, British, and Jordanian administrations through to Israeli military rule since 1967. As traveling from and to Nablus is difficult for Arabs from the region, the city constitutes an encapsulated place with a strong character.

Nablus is inhabited by small minorities of Christians and Samaritans, but the majority of its residents are Sunni Muslims who ascribe different degrees of importance to Islam in their lives.[14] References to the Quran and Islamic concepts shape private and public interactions in this city, which has a long-standing reputation as a conservative place (Doumani 1995) with excellent soap factories (Bontemps 2012). Regardless of religious affiliation, the inhabitants of Nablus have formed a close-knit community under military occupation. People try to live a good life in community with others, often against the grain of an opaque and repressive political regime.

Nablus became a stronghold of Palestinian militants affiliated with Hamas or Fatah during the Second Intifada. Below the old city are myriad catacombs and water canals, in which the young men who fought against the Israeli army moved and hid during this second uprising. Israeli generals responded by developing a street-fighting tactic known as "walking through walls." That is, they cut through floors and walls so they could move their armed forces unpredictably throughout the city (Weizman 2006). Combined with a military siege and air raids, such tactics damaged several parts of the old city center. Everybody who could afford to do so has since moved to newer developments, and the city has continued to expand up the northern and southern mountain slopes.

When the Second Intifada ended in 2006, many of the insurgents who had fought in Nablus were executed or imprisoned by the Israeli military. Others received amnesty provided they joined the PA security forces operating under the tutelage of the Israeli army and funded by the United States and Europe (International Crisis Group 2008; Tartir 2019). The pictures of many fighters remain visible on public posters throughout the city, and several small shrines in the old city remember the names of young men and the places where they faced death. Meanwhile, Hamas has retained an important presence in Nablus in opposition to the Fatah-dominated PA in Ramallah. Many of the politically important families in Nablus have had "Hamas" spray-painted at the entries of their reception halls (diwans) used for wedding feasts and funerals (Doumani 1998, 31).[15]

At the time of my fieldwork, the political mood in the city was one of discouragement. The hopes for Palestinian statehood, which had gained steam in the 1980s through to the early 2000s, had partly cooled down as Israeli settlements surrounding the city continued to expand.[16] Israeli military bases on both the northern and southern mountains overlooked the city and the adjacent Palestinian refugee camps of Balata and 'Ayn Beit al-Ma'. Very few people living in Nablus were able to obtain permits allowing them to commute from Nablus to work in Tel Aviv, a car journey that takes less than an hour. Israeli occupation disconnected the inhabitants of Nablus from Palestinians living in the Gaza Strip and from the Palestinians with Israeli citizenship living "inside" (*juwwa*) the borders of 1967, the "Arabs of Israel."[17]

The main travel destination for residents of Nablus was Ramallah, which connects the city with Jerusalem and the southern West Bank. While employees of the new public sector in Ramallah have increasingly enjoyed an upper-middle-class lifestyle, many people in other parts of the West Bank still struggle to make ends meet. The inhabitants of Nablus thus tended to frown on Ramallah as a more secularized part of Palestine and to resent its wealth amounting from its position as the focal point of international aid.[18] The Israeli siege during the Second Intifada had not only isolated Nablus from the rest of Palestine but also destroyed most of its industry. Nablus had subsequently become more dependent on the wider economy of international aid in the Palestinian territories, which primarily translated into salaries for public servants and employees of the city's Najah University. Such aid flows are erratic and tied to political conditions. Ever since 2007, international aid to Palestine has come under intense political scrutiny by governmental authorities seeking to undermine any political or militant activism against the Israeli occupation. Monetary aid is generally channeled toward those segments of Palestinian society that acquiesce to settlement expansion (Challand 2009). Against this background, foreign aid has had a divisive effect on the Palestinian population, creating winners and losers (Turner 2014, 46–47), with the city of Nablus largely on the losing end. Zakat institutions to a certain extent fill this gap by providing social welfare to Palestinians throughout the occupied territories.

The Political Economy of Zakat Institutions in Palestine

In the absence of a functioning state welfare system, local and transnational zakat flows have given rise to organized structures of community support, channeling cash and food donations to beneficiaries, coordinating benevolent loans issued by Islamic banks, and running social projects in Palestine. In the 1970s, Palestinians in the occupied territories began establishing a wide range of official zakat institutions. Informal committees associated with particular mosques in the West Bank began pooling local zakat donations, then sought legal registration as "zakat committees."[19] Such legal registration allowed them to open international bank accounts and gradually obtain access to international zakat funds coming from the Arab Gulf States and Muslim communities in Europe and North America, as well as regular nongovernmental organization (NGO) funding from the US Agency for International Development (USAID) and the European Union. These zakat institutions then sponsored programs to support orphans and families and develop soup kitchens, medical clinics, hospitals, schools, Quranic literacy centers, job-creation projects, and labor-advocacy agencies. Their regular cash transfers to local communities, along with their apparent independence from the political agendas of aid agencies, earned the zakat committees the trust of the local public (Hilal and Maliki

1997; Lundblad 2008; Schaeublin 2020). Most Palestinians perceived these institutions as part of a wider socioeconomic landscape of community support intended to enhance local steadfastness and encourage people to hold on to their land in the face of continued Israeli settlement expansion (Ishtiyya 2008; Schaeublin 2009, 23).

After the establishment of the Palestinian Authority, Arafat's policy toward zakat committees reflected the need to integrate local structures of governance into preparations for Palestinian statehood. His strategy toward local zakat committees was similar to his policy of partly co-opting informal justice (*iṣlāḥ*) committees. In 1994, Arafat issued a decree establishing a department of tribal affairs within the president's office that oversaw informal justice committees. Arafat thereby sought to exercise political control over justice procedures operating outside a state framework by granting informal justice committees an official status and letting them carry on with their work (D. Khalidi et al., 2006, 59, 90–91).[20]

In the aftermath of the September 11, 2001, attacks in New York and Washington, DC, the US government increasingly perceived Islamic institutions worldwide as a threat because of their alleged connections to Islamic militant groups. The Palestinian zakat institutions were no exception. The US government and the families of people that had fallen victim to violent attacks carried out by Hamas in Israel alleged zakat committees to be fronts for Hamas and took their international donors and banks to court (Benthall 2016). Hamas had been listed as a terrorist organization in the United States since 1997 because it had used violence to derail the peace process and Hamas's armed forces had been central to the Israeli-Palestinian confrontations of the Second Intifada.

As Nablus is a former stronghold of armed insurgents, its residents have continued to live under a surveillance regime imposed by the Israeli army and PA security forces. When I was there in 2013 and 2014, Israeli armed forces regularly patrolled its streets. Intelligence services exerted control over the entire Palestinian population by co-opting parts of it and relying on webs of local informants. Politically active Palestinians, such as students at the University of Nablus, were commonly arrested and interrogated.[21] Any relationship between Hamas and the zakat sector also became a question of utmost sensitivity, with court cases having a chilling effect (James 2019b) on Islamic giving from the United States to conflict zones with Muslim populations in need.

In 2008, the PA implemented political reforms intended to exert centralized control over aid flowing into the West Bank. Giving in to international pressures, the PA resorted to heavy-handed interventions in the zakat sector, forcing dozens of committees—including those in and around Nablus—to close. After confiscating their properties, the PA created new centralized committees under its direct political control. Nablus locals did not trust the new committee set up for their city, because they thought its members were too close to the PA, which they viewed as corrupt. Consequently, more zakat was given directly to the needy without going through an intermediary institution. Nablus residents have depended on such informal support from their relatives or neighbors ever since. However, by the time I moved to Nablus in 2013, some of its residents had composed a new zakat committee with people known for their integrity and their distance from the Palestinian Authority. To regain popular confidence, the new zakat committee members endeavored to demonstrate their piety and ability to handle zakat donations appropriately under the critical observation and ethical judgment of the people of Nablus.

Unfortunately, such local mechanisms for holding Islamic socioeconomic structures accountable are poorly understood in scholarly debates and among international policy makers. Mechanisms based on the cultivation of local reputations and lateral disciplining stand in stark contrast to counterterrorist surveillance agencies pressuring foreign zakat donors and banks to use global security databases and "terror lists" to vet the board members of local committees and screen their beneficiaries before transferring any money to them (James 2019b). This book adopts an anthropological approach to filling this gap by providing a study of Islam in everyday interactions and documenting how accountability through the embodiment and display of virtues and the cultivation of reputation works in Nablus. Against this background, I analyze the potential and the limits of lateral disciplining and accountability through reputation when it comes to economic power relations under military occupation.

The Arc of This Book

Minor acts of disciplining in seemingly mundane, day-to-day interactions enforce social duties of care and underpin ways of holding people accountable. Providing an empirical study of how people in Nablus negotiate situations of material scarcity and the obligation to support those in need, this book analyzes how references to the Islamic scriptures and invocations of God constitute social interactions as a field of ethical practice. This provides the practical framework in which zakat and sadaqa giving unfolds and where zakat gains its quality as divine money. Putting social interactions at the center, the book challenges the exceptionalism that continues to drive scholarly and journalistic writings on social life in the Arabic-speaking Middle East. It shows that by referencing Islamic concepts, people in Nablus address a paradox that is hardly unique to the Middle East: the contradiction between an ideal of moral equality and the actual existence of hierarchies of wealth. In any society, the flow of wealth is embedded in a field of interaction wherein people invoke ethical concepts to structure personal acts of giving, commercial transactions, and social institutions and seek to make them transparent and morally accountable to the community.

Chapter 1 discusses ethical and methodological questions regarding ethnographic research on zakat practices based on long-term fieldwork in Nablus. It makes my positionality in the field transparent to the reader and documents my attempts to become respectable in the city by learning to navigate face-to-face interactions and subjecting myself to the lateral disciplining of others.

Chapter 2 provides an overview of the historical trajectory of the Nablus Zakat Committee (NZC) established in the 1970s. Operating within an evolving legal framework, the committee eventually became a model for the redistribution of charitable funds that was replicated across the region. In the course of the United States' self-declared war on terror, zakat committees in the West Bank came under pressure for alleged links to Hamas and faced security crackdowns starting in 2007. At the time of my fieldwork, new members of the NZC were attempting to regain the confidence of the local population. To do so, they had to embody Islamic virtues in their interactions with others and cultivate a good reputation.

Moving on from these historical and institutional analyses, the next chapters turn to informal zakat practices. Chapter 3 discusses how people in situations of acute material need navigate everyday economic interactions, including direct zakat transactions, while avoiding shame and retaining their dignity. This requires them to pay delicate attention to concealing and exposing their needs at the right moments and with the appropriate signs. Building on these insights, chapter 4 analyzes how zakat givers detect the financial needs of people who seek to conceal them and explores the gestures and sayings with which they seek to preserve the dignity of the recipients. This leads into an analysis of the two models of zakat in action. Invoking God as the Ultimate Provider of wealth allows givers to depersonalize their gifts and thereby enact zakat as a transaction of divine money. At the same time, givers often calculate what they owe to God in terms of zakat and assume that He will reward them for their gifts.

Expanding on this analysis of interactions between givers and receivers of zakat, chapter 5 examines how the ethics of giving, evocations of shame and honor, and the idea of God as Divine Arbiter and Ultimate Provider of wealth also emerge in market transactions. An Islamic public culture sustained by invocations of God in greetings and on countless stickers and posters embeds market activity in an ethical field. In this context, people sometimes deploy conceptions of God as divine bookkeeper or provider that correspond to the two models of zakat described above in order to laterally discipline merchants who are trying to cultivate a reputation for piety.

Chapter 6 explores the ethical dilemmas and contradictions arising in a political economy of long-term occupation and discusses why many people in Nablus hold on to the idea of a divine system of moral accounting and reward. The idea of an invisible other world that is constantly brought in touch with this world (during funerals, for instance) allows people to hold on to an idea of ultimate justice and pursue a good ethical life in community with others while making a living in the midst of a repressive and opaque political landscape. God figures in stories that seek to encourage people to cultivate piety in spite of adverse circumstance, while discouraging them from engaging in illicit dealings such as usury. Turning to the wider political economy and the Palestinian capitalist class, this final chapter discusses the limits of lateral disciplining based on Islamic concepts when it comes to challenging economic power relations in Palestine and in the wider Middle East. Finally, the insights from the ethnography presented in this book are put into the wider perspective of Arab countries after the revolutions of 2011 where many governments still fail to provide effective social safety nets to their populations.

1

Fieldwork under Military Rule

Subjecting Oneself to Lateral Disciplining

Anthropologists gain knowledge about the world through their bodies. They immerse themselves in unfamiliar social milieus, adopting new habits, enacting new gestures, showing respect in new ways, and possibly developing a new sense of humor. This process of being unsettled in one's assumptions and habitual forms of inhabiting the world is part of the research process. This chapter documents my own process of trying to become a respectable person in Nablus in an attempt to make the process of anthropological knowledge production—as I conducted it—transparent to the reader. Starting from my entry into the field of zakat practices in Nablus, I discuss considerations about research ethics under military occupation that informed my choices in the field. Subsequently, I trace my process of learning to become a respectful and respected person in this context by subjecting myself to being disciplined by the people around me.

Entering the Field of Zakat Practices in Nablus

Before starting this ethnographic research project on zakat practices in Nablus, I had conducted short field studies on the zakat sector in the West Bank (Schaeublin 2009) and the Gaza Strip (Schaeublin 2012) in the context of a wider research project at the Graduate Institute of International and Development Studies in Geneva. This project set out to test the proposition that counterterrorist policies targeting Islamic aid flows were an overreaction. The task of documenting the crackdown waged against Islamic social institutions in the West Bank allowed me to listen to a variety of different views on zakat and how it should be properly organized according to Islamic precepts. Both the people driven out of the zakat committees and those enforcing the closures were willing to meet me and share their perspective on the issue. After translating my studies into Arabic, I presented them to different academic audiences in the West Bank and in the Gaza Strip.

I arrived in Nablus in 2013 as a lone ethnographer with the aim of understanding acts of giving and references to Islamic scriptures and God in everyday interactions. By that time, I had adopted what James Laidlaw (2014, 46) calls an "ethnographic stance" in the study of ethical practices: "taking seriously the forms of life we describe: regarding them—and therefore describing them—as something we learn from as well as about.... [Moreover, this stance] involves learning to think with as well as about its concepts, such that they become resources in our own critical reflection and self-constitution."

Having previously studied Arabic in Geneva, Birzeit (a Palestinian university), Sanaʿa, and Damascus, I was fluent in both classical and colloquial Arabic when I arrived in Nablus. Accordingly, I found it relatively easy to integrate Islamic concepts into my analytical way of thinking. My ethnographic focus on interactions (in Arabic, I would speak of *muʿāmalāt*) turned out to be feasible and productive.

By the time I arrived in Nablus in 2013, my published work on zakat in Palestine had become available in Arabic (Schaeublin 2009a, 2012a). This made my research agenda more transparent to people living in the occupied Palestinian territories. It also helped me obtain the support of a former member of the Nablus Zakat Committee (NZC), Adly Yaish, for my project. Yaish served several terms as mayor of Nablus, one before and one after my fieldwork. In spite of his support, my first attempts to establish working relations with the official NZC proved difficult. I initially filled my time wandering the city, greeting people, making friends, and entering into lengthy conversations. I always explained my presence in Nablus as a researcher studying how people cope with wealth and poverty in zakat interactions. Countless informal conversations, the situations I observed, and evenings spent in the company of many different people have nourished the descriptions and thoughts presented in this book.

As I gradually gained a respected reputation in Nablus, zakat donors started taking me along on visits to poor households. The NZC had been recomposed with new members just before the beginning of my fieldwork and had started to regain the trust of the inhabitants of the city. Over time, they let me take part in their activities and conduct roughly one hundred interviews with current and former members of the committee overseeing the collection and distribution of zakat funds, Islamic scholars advising others on the practice of giving and receiving, and Palestinian authority officials in charge of governing zakat institutions. Moreover, I talked to local archivists and zakat activists about the historical evolution of zakat in Palestine and cultivated personal relations and friendships with several neighbors, day laborers, sheikhs, market sellers, and people in financially challenging situations. In my attempt to socialize with people from different social classes, I paid several visits to Munib al-Masri, possibly the richest inhabitant of Nablus, who lived in a mansion on the southern hill. I also collected stickers and posters with Islamic concepts and sayings, in addition to legal documents and leaflets on zakat and audio files of radio shows on zakat practice in Nablus. I interviewed Islamic scholars across the West Bank in various positions (mufti, imam, administrator, professors at sharia faculties). Most of them seemed more interested in the theological aspects of Islamic giving. Some of them, however, referred me to a guidebook written by a group of scholars (Nablus Zakat Committee 2001) that provides practical advice on the gestures and attitudes required in the pious giving and receiving of zakat and sadaqa.

Before starting to take part in zakat practices, however, I needed to negotiate my presence in the field and find my role as an ethnographer. On this level, I confronted a number of ethical constraints and challenges while conducting fieldwork in a city under military occupation.

Ethical Considerations about Participant Observation under Military Occupation

One of the ethical problems that arises in the encounter between ethnographers and the people among whom they conduct research is how to handle economic and power inequalities (T. Asad 1973). I tried to be as aware as possible of the power relations within which my research project—as an act of knowledge production—was unfolding. In my case, a racialized security landscape sustained this imbalance of power. While I could move freely, the people I lived with could not. This was partly a matter of my looks as a white European and of my passport. These personal characteristics made crossing borders or checkpoints and moving within Israeli and Palestinian public space generally easy. In the West Bank, however, these qualities also nourished certain suspicions. My appearance as a whitey (*ajnabī*) arriving in Nablus with an openly stated interest in conducting research on zakat raised many eyebrows. Most foreigners were coming to the city as scattered tourists, researchers from European or American universities, or people working on projects for nongovernmental organizations or the Nablus office of the International Committee of the Red Cross. In the years prior to my fieldwork, people were spreading rumors that spies mingled with groups of white foreigners. Allegedly, they were gathering information on the Palestinian population in order to share it with Israeli, European, or American intelligence services.[1]

Extended families or clans in Nablus have considerable political weight as people rely on their family networks when confronted with conflicts and legal issues (D. Khalidi et al. 2006). However, researching the political dynamics of families was impossible from my ethnographic position. In a city already overburdened with intelligence surveillance, there was no decent way to study local power structures—at least not without damaging my local reputation. Questions regarding the politics or size of families immediately reminded my interlocutors of conversations they had had with Israeli intelligence officers during interrogations. I am grateful to my interlocutors who explained this to me in all openness, whether they said it jokingly or with a serious face. Local power networks are thus a blind spot of this book.[2]

The omnipresent concern with family honor also made any inquiry into informal zakat giving very challenging. Recipients of zakat were extremely hesitant to talk about the topic because revealing their need to others might expose them and bring shame on their family or extended relatives. Rather than studying zakat beneficiaries, I focused my research on the discreet ways in which givers of zakat detected signs of need in their surroundings and met them without damaging the honorable reputations of recipients and their families.

I was similarly constrained from interacting with women in Nablus because of my gender. With few exceptions, such as at university campuses, expensive cafés, and gatherings with relatives, most events in people's everyday lives are highly segregated by gender. This constraint was exacerbated in my case by the reputation for loose morals that white foreigners have acquired in Nablus. According to a popular view, white foreigners (especially women) were spreading debauchery in the local population to weaken Palestinian steadfastness and resistance. The Palestinian novel entitled *Blonde Ramallah* (Yahiya 2013), which amplifies such accusations, enjoyed wide currency in Nablus. Being a man, a white man in particular, thus limited my ethnographic access to women.

To provide a counterweight to this bias, I employed a woman research assistant, Marah Az, to whom I had been introduced by a mutual friend from Gaza City. Marah joined several women's gatherings and conducted interviews with eight women of different ages and backgrounds on how they practice zakat and sadaqa. As in the cafés, markets, and streets where men mingle, these gatherings constitute public spheres, where the public gaze is present and felt.[3] Marah's mother was active in direct giving. Marah went through her personal networks to contact other women representing different ages and financial situations. Some had middle-class jobs. Others were widows living off the funds their deceased husbands had left them. Some relied on the financial assistance of their sons. Marah suspected that they sometimes provided only limited information because of the secrecy surrounding zakat transfers. Her observations and interviews, however, provide a nuanced picture of the discretion and caution surrounding direct practices of giving. I draw on Marah's observations and the statements made by these different women to reconstruct interactions between women giving and receiving zakat. Marah and I regularly met at closing time at the travel agency where she worked to discuss her findings. I am deeply indebted to her for her insights and diligent work on behalf of this project.

When conducting ethnographic research, being transparent about one's own ethical commitments is crucial for maintaining one's integrity. Interlocutors might read participation in certain forms of religious practice as a signal of conversion. Such assumptions can give rise to accusations of hypocrisy (Clarke 2013). In a world of global connectivity, it is no longer possible to convert in the field and then, after one leaves, undo the conversion without facing serious consequences.[4] Knowing that interlocutors might interpret participation in Muslim practices as a religious commitment, I refrained from joining others in prayer and consistently admitted that I was not Muslim throughout my time in the field. When people asked why I would not join them in prayer, I said that doing so would turn me into a liar; this explanation seemed to gain me respect in some cases. However, as I increasingly participated in social interactions in Nablus, my neighbors and friends introduced me to appropriate ways of greeting and behaving in the presence of others. I gradually realized the central role ascribed to Islamic concepts in greetings and polite speech. It was impossible to entertain respectful social relations without taking part in an elaborate system of greetings and countergreetings, wishes and counterwishes, acts of giving and taking.

Initially, I was a little ambivalent about using Islamic phrases or concepts when participating in ordinary social interactions. I finally decided to reciprocate Islamic greetings with invocations of God to bless the people with whom I spoke or express my gratitude to God in those situations where this was expected. A friend in Nablus observed the tension arising from this: "You are always interacting with people in an Islamic way, saying 'Praise be to God (*al-ḥamdu li-llah*)' when they ask you how you are doing. People like this a lot, but why are you doing this if you are not a Muslim?"

I answered that I appreciate taking part in Islamic interactions (*muʿāmalāt*) and that I would like to learn from these practices without, however, becoming a Muslim. Throughout my fieldwork, this was a good enough answer. No one interpreted this as a malicious attempt at pretending to be Muslim. Most of my interlocutors appreciated this as respectful behavior, not hypocrisy. As a religious skeptic (i.e., somebody who recognizes prophets and the ways in which they have reshaped social life but questions how humans have institutionalized their messages), I could reconcile such interchanges with my convictions. Moreover, such participation allowed me to explore lived Islamic practice and the presence of God within human encounters, especially zakat interchanges.

Participation in such interactions had both disciplining and enabling effects on me. It affected my constitution as a person and gave me more confidence as I moved through the city. As I became increasingly aware that people observed my movements, gestures, statements, transactions, and interactions closely, I went through a process of becoming worthy of respect. Virtues such as relying on God for one's future well-being became part of the way in which I experienced social life. This transformation of habitus was easily reconciled with my "vocation" as an anthropologist (Lévi-Strauss 1973, 55). Doing research for this book thus required I subject myself to discipline by others in social interactions as I actively sought to cultivate a good moral reputation in Nablus.

Becoming Respectable in Nablus

On a walk in Nablus shortly after my arrival in the city, I stopped at a tiny place selling drinks and sandwiches and exchanged greetings with the shopkeeper, a man by the name of Ahmed, who wore a dapper shirt. He invited me to sit in the back of his shop and offered me a cup of coffee, while he continued to take care of his customers. Over his shoulder, Ahmed asked me what I had come to do in Nablus. I told him that I was a researcher intending to live here for a year in order to understand life in this city and that I was particularly interested in poverty and Islamic alms (zakat). He looked surprised. I mentioned that the former mayor of Nablus, Adly Yaish, supported my project. Ahmed told me that he had a place a few hundred meters from his shop on the slope of the city's northern hill and that he would like to rent it out. It turned out to be an old, abandoned house (fig. 1.1). We agreed on me paying two months of rent in advance and him renovating and furnishing a list of things before I would move in. We wrote it all down on a small piece of paper and added our signatures. Ahmed said that the renovation would take a month. I shook his hand to seal the deal and said goodbye. Ahmed ended the conversation by commanding me to rely on God (*tawakkal 'alā allah*).

For the period of the renovation, I moved into another apartment in a neighborhood on the slope of the southern hill of Nablus. One night on my way

Figure 1.1. The author sitting on the porch on the ground floor of the old house, fronted by a little garden. An apartment building carried by concrete pillars sits atop it. © Iwan Schauwecker

home, a group of young men approached me. Forming a circle around me in a slightly intimidating way, they asked me what I was doing there and invited me to have tea with them. On a small concrete terrace overlooking one of the main streets winding up the southern mountain, they asked me questions concerning my political views and my personal life. I told them a lot about myself—my experiences growing up, the love relations I had had in my life, my insecurities regarding my position as a researcher in Nablus. This appeared to disperse some of their suspicions. I suspect that some of the people interviewing me early on in my fieldwork might have reported what I told them to branches of the Palestinian secret services.

A few weeks later, I moved into my new place. To reach it, I had to mount a steep one-way alley leading into a quiet neighborhood on the northern hill. When I moved in, my landlord, Ahmed, had filled the entire place with sofas. Being hardly able to move in the apartment because of these sofas, I asked him to remove some of them again. There was also a framed image on the wall exposing the ninety-nine names of God in golden letters. Ahmed left me a large pot of olives and plenty of tea bags in the kitchen—for hosting neighbors and friends. Moreover, he placed a copy of the Quran in the house, in order to protect the place. Finally, he showed me an ancient radio that was tuned to the local Quran Radio station. Ahmed recommended that I listen to it often, as it would have a relaxing effect on the heart.

In this place, I started hosting and visiting neighbors and learned how to navigate face-to-face interactions in a respectful way. In Nablus, the term *respect* (*iḥtirām*) stands for the ability to handle encounters in a way that is attentive to the public appearance of another. Being respectable (*muḥtaram*) means being sensitive to both (1) how the person one interacts with appears, especially when a third party is watching, and (2) how the person effectively feels—that is, what he or she might really want or need. Developing these skills was crucial for my acceptance as a person.[5] Learning such lessons began when people started coming over to my place.

The Duty of Hosting and Visiting

Male neighbors and friends frequently came over to see me in my ground-floor apartment. They often brought me a plate of the food cooked by the women in their families, such as lentil soup or meat with okra and tomatoes. In turn, they taught me to be a good host. I learned from them what food and beverages I should provide and how to greet and say farewell to my visitors appropriately. When people knocked on my door, I usually invited them to come in by saying, "Be so kind as to enter (*tafaḍḍalū*)." Asking them to sit down on sofas laid out in a circle, I offered coffee or tea with nuts, seeds, or cookies. At the first moment of silence in the conversation, I would say, "You are welcome (*ahlan wa sahlan*)!" I observed this practice when visiting other people and came to understand the expression as a way of marking the "space of hospitality" (Shryock 2012, 24).

Hosting people who arrived unexpectedly taught me to give my full attention and openness to the presence of my guests. After serving tea (preferably very dark, as light tea in Nablus signaled meanness), I leaned back, relaxed, and engaged in the conversation. Sometimes, I felt my body being pulled into the chair, preventing me from expressing any sign of impatience that might suggest to my guests that I could have something else to do. The more I learned about hosting, the more I enjoyed opening such a window in time, sitting with neighbors or friends. After a certain amount of time, which varied from twenty to thirty minutes, I usually offered to make another round of tea or coffee. The conversation continued all along.

On hearing my guests mention that they were thinking of leaving, I learned to insist several times that they should stay by repeating what I had heard in other people's homes: "It is too early to leave!" or "Keep yourself here (*khallī-k*)!" or "After the coffee!" When one of my visitors finally left my place, we would exchange the following good wishes:

Neighbor: "My dear (*ḥabībī inta*)!"
Me: "You are dear to me (*inta ḥabībī*)!"

Neighbor: "God give you health (*allah yaʿatī-k al-ʿāfiya*)!"
Me: "May God make you healthy (*allah yaʿafī-k*)!"

Neighbor: "God animate you (*ḥayyā-k allah*)!"
Me: "May God animate you (*allah yaḥyī-k*)!"

Neighbor: "Wake up to [a day] of kindheartedness (*tiṣbaḥ ʿala al-khayr*)!" [The expression is used to say good night.]
Me: "And may you be among the people of the kindheartedness (*wa inta min ahl-hu*)!"

Once they left the house and were slowly walking away, my visitors would throw the following question at my door to mark the final moment of parting: "Do you need anything (*bidd-ak shī*)?" I was expected to reply: "Your well-being (*salāmt-ak*)!"

Ayman, a man in his early sixties, was one of my most frequent guests. He often knocked on my door in the evening. After having tea and exchanging the latest news on weddings and funerals in the neighborhood, he sometimes fell asleep on one of my sofas. His presence brought a soothing calm into my home, and Ayman occasionally commented that he found my house an excellent place to relax. One day he told me that coming over to his house for a spontaneous visit, with or without the company of others, was my right (*ḥaqq*) as a neighbor. Ayman instructed me that, from an Islamic perspective, visiting neighbors and asking after them increases your good deeds (*ḥasanāt*) and will get you recompense (*thawāb*) in the Hereafter. If you were to neglect your neighbors, you would risk one of them going to bed with an empty stomach. Ayman cited a saying (*ḥadīth*) ascribed to the Prophet stating that such an occurrence has a negative influence on the divine account of good deeds of everybody living in the surrounding houses.

As a guest, I learned to avoid thanking my hosts too ostentatiously and to conduct myself in a way that would depersonalize the gift. After sharing a meal at somebody's place, for instance, one usually wishes the person who has offered the food, "God willing you [you will] always [be able to offer this] (*in shāʾ allah dāʾima*)." This suggests that God is the real source providing the meal and that the host is merely a channel for His provisions. When friends invited me to stay at their place, they would often refuse to be "thanked" for their hospitality. When I thanked them (as my parents raised me to do), they sometimes gave me bewildered looks and said, "There is no thank-you between us (*mā fī shukran bayn-nā*)."

These daily interactions gave me a sense of stability and security. I hosted a variety of guests, listening to their stories and disclosing many personal details about my own life. I learned how to treat people politely and grew emotionally attached to a number of people in my surroundings. At the same time, I became more and more aware that my neighbors were watching me and interpreting my movements and actions. For example, after I had been living in the new neighborhood for a few weeks, an older man approached me and informed me that he had an important position around there. He added that, in the beginning, he had been skeptical about my presence but then he heard from other people that I was a good guy (*inna-k mnīḥ*). In the evening, I told a friend about this incident. He exclaimed, "Who does that man think he is?" This reaction surprised me. It seemed that most people did not appreciate other people's attempts to present themselves as authority figures. This taught me that being a respectable person also required not subordinating oneself and not letting other people tell you what to do. Exposing good demeanor (*akhlāq*) helps one gain a reputation as a respectful person, but it does not suffice to demonstrate that one is also respected for one's autonomy.

Navigating Mutual Support

Becoming a respectable neighbor went along with developing relations of mutual support. When I had occasion to travel to the adjacent country of Jordan to renew my visa, I often brought back things such as baby milk powder, cigarettes, or medications that my neighbors or friends had asked me to get because they were more expensive in the West Bank. Sometimes, people paid me for these orders. At other times, they took the goods and told me that they would pay later. Asking for the money after a lapse of time was tricky. It felt uncomfortable to bring up the issue. When I hesitatingly did so, they sometimes gave me a part of the sum, accompanied by an explanation that they were under financial pressure (*maḍghūṭ*). Instead of giving me money, some of my neighbors would continue to bring me simple food from their households, such as lentil soup, yogurt, olives, or two loaves of fresh bread. My neighbors would also look out for me by informing me about what was happening in the neighborhood, such as when Israeli soldiers began running local nightly arrest operations. In return, I was sometimes asked to attempt to fix a neighbor's sink or transport furniture.

People often read spontaneous or all-too-lavish giving as an attempt to subordinate them. This makes giving among neighbors and friends a sensitive issue. Consider this example of how a minor gift of food led to tensions at a mourning feast after a funeral in a village near Nablus. On a sunny day in February, I reached the farm where the mourning feast was taking place. After I gave my condolences to the family, someone guided me to a stone terrace next to an olive grove. There were about twenty men sitting around plastic tables. After shaking hands with all of them, I sat down at one of these tables. After a while, young men started putting large round aluminum plates, called ṣidr, in the midst of each table. Cooked lamb lay on top of a mountain of rice. A few minutes later, a young man brought a pot of *sharāb*, a yogurt sauce, which he poured over the rice and the meat. Now, the two men at my table and I started to eat slowly and silently from the same plate using spoons. The solemn expressions on our faces were appropriate to the mood of a funeral. We ate from different sides of the large plate, digging three different wells into the rice. At some stage, a young man came with more *sharāb* and poured it over the rice, filling the holes in front of us and turning them into three small ponds.

By now, each of us had eaten one of the meat pieces, which were scattered on top of the rice. Suddenly, the man to my left used his spoon to push another chunk of meat into the lake in front of me. I did not quite know how to react. I did not want to fish the chunk of meat out of my lake and put it back, even though I felt embarrassed by the situation and recognized that accepting the gift could be read as a sign of subordination. Apparently out of pity for my having been put in a subordinate position, the man to my right then pushed a chunk of meat into the lake of the man to my left, who immediately started protesting: "No, I do not want this." He tried to give it back to the other man, who responded by saying the same thing: "No, I do not want this." In the end, the man to my left used his hands to tear the chunk of meat apart into pieces and tossed some of them into the lake of the other man and some of them into his own zone in this landscape of food. Slowly, everyone relaxed again and continued sharing the meal while moving on to casual conversation.

This incident taught me a lesson on how to push back against gestures that could be read as an attempt to put me in a subordinate position. Learning how to navigate such situations turned out to be key to becoming both a respectful and a respected person. I gradually stopped accepting when traders offered goods to me using such expressions as "Keep this one on us," "I don't want to take money from you," or "This is from me." Refusing such offers required me to insist on paying, albeit in a discreet way. I would slip coins on a counter without attracting any attention, while engaging in jocular, "light-blooded" (*khafīf al-damm*) conversation. This made the payment appear to be incidental, a method that worked well and helped me to be taken more seriously in the markets and to gain a reputation as a respectable man (*rajul muḥtaram*). It also prevented such interactions from escalating into competitions over who is able to assert his or her autonomy at the expense of subordinating the other, as discussed in more detail in later chapters.

Among friends, depersonalizing small gifts made them lose their offensive quality. When spending time in a café in company, openly splitting the bill for drinks was often unthinkable. If one wanted to pay, one could sneak to the counter and pay one's own drinks discreetly. Sometimes, I covered the entire bill without telling others. In this case, I needed to shake off the protests of my friends by jokingly downplaying my role in the transactions and quickly changing the subject of conversation.

Islam and Lateral Disciplining

Making social interactions the central focus of my ethnographic work allowed me to understand them as a field of Islamic ethical practice, wherein people laterally discipline one another. My friends denied certain forms of lateral disciplining, especially attempts at correcting the behavior of someone in the presence of others, as unduly intrusive (*tadakhul*).[6] When a young man in a café started asking me about my religious beliefs in front of others, for instance, one of my friends pulled me aside. He told me that I should not tolerate such intrusion and questioning of my conduct in front of others. One afternoon, I agreed to host a female journalist at my place. As we passed my landlord's shop on our way there, I introduced her to him. When we reached my place, my journalist friend started working on her laptop. Soon thereafter, my landlord called me, demanding that this woman leave my apartment immediately. When I discussed this event later with friends, they told me that I should never have stopped at the shop with her as this attracted the attention not only of my landlord but also of bystanders. They advised being discreet about anything that slightly deviated from the generally expected moral behavior. One of them said that he lived according to this saying: "Dress according to the taste of the people but eat according to your own taste [*ilbis 'alā dhū' an-nās, bas kul 'alā dhū'-ak inta*]." This suggests that occasional concealment can be a necessary part of leading a respectable life. This is how certain people in Nablus, for instance, went about drinking alcohol. They bought it in liquor shops from a Samaritan village on the southern hill, transported it in dark plastic bags in the trunks of their cars, and drank it in their apartments. While alcohol consumption was much more accepted in Nablus in the past, there seemed to be a consensus at the time of my fieldwork that drinking could occur as long as it was concealed from the public gaze.

Ethical disciplining took more subtle forms in everyday interactions. Most greetings and countergreetings in Nablus invoke God and His ability to sustain people. Learning and practicing them on a daily basis, I realized that such greetings have a disciplinary effect. Using them constantly reminds oneself to rely on God and not to take pride in one's own acts and achievements. At a certain point, I made a conscious decision to go along with this process and let myself by laterally disciplined by others through this everyday practice of greeting. Doing so meant I would not only attend to my respectability but also actively embody piety in my encounters with others.

Several transmitted sayings of the Prophet highlight the importance of greeting as a central part of practicing Islam, even if it does not involve the transaction of anything material.[7] In Nablus, most greetings contain a wish that God may bring good things to the other person. Greeting someone in the street, one can say, "May God give you health [*allah ya'atī-k al-'āfiya*]." This greeting requires a standard response: "May God keep you healthy [*allah ya'afī-k*]." Most expressions have a defined countergreeting, which contains the same content as the initial greeting in a slightly modified articulation. In cases where there are no defined countergreetings, it is possible to simply offer a standard reply such as "May God support you [*allah ys'ad-ak*]" or "May God sustain you [*allah ykhallī-k*]."

When asked how I was doing, I would often simply say, "The praise is to God [*al-ḥamdu li-llah*]." Pronounced with the right tone and facial expression, this statement is commonly interpreted as a sign of piety signaling one's reliance on God. When one senses that someone else is having a hard time, it is polite to say, "May God provide you with His provision [*allah yrziq-ak*]" or "May God make you achieve your aspirations [*allah ywaffq-ak*]." When somebody joins a group standing in the street, one can say, "The blessing has come down (upon us) [*ḥallat al-baraka ('alay-nā)*]." To strangers arriving to the city, one can say, "You are illuminating [*inta munawwir*] Nablus" or, simplified, "You have illuminated [*nawwart*] (the place)." These statements laud people for carrying divine blessing or divine light.

Sometimes those without a stable income display piety to laterally discipline middle-class people. An example is the expression "May God animate you [*ḥayā-k allah*]," used in greetings. I heard several pious lower-class people use it in public interactions with Palestinians from the more secularized middle class. Sometimes the tone of voice suggested that the speakers were presenting themselves as persons who, in spite of living in difficult conditions, maintained their faith. At the same time, they seemed to hint that their middle-class counterparts might have lost connection to this type of faith. Having a steady income, they might have forgotten what it means to rely on God.

Palestinian Christians use some but not all of the Islamic greetings. Arab Christians told me that they respond to greetings viewed as being explicitly Islamic with the appropriate countergreeting but that they would not use them in the first place. Instead, they tended to use greetings not directly associated with Islam, such as "good morning/evening" or "welcome [*ahlan wa sahlan*]" or "We thank God [*nshkur allah*]." I did not learn such subtle ways of communicating a Christian identity in social interactions. However, such an endeavor could turn into fascinating ethnographic research on social interactions in the region.[8]

Cultivating one's ethical self-worth in interactions foremost consists of repeatedly expressing in public interactions that one relies on God (*tawakkal 'alā allah*). Reliance on God (*tawakkul*) is a virtue that is cultivated in different ways. It starts with the omnipresent addition of the expression "God willing [*in shā allah*]" when speaking to others about any future event. Moreover, it is common to say "In the name of God [*bismillah*]" or "Oh Lord [*yā rabb*]" before starting a car or walking through a door. Merchants and customers tend to seal deals that involve future actions with the expression "Let us rely on God [*tawakkal-nā 'alā allah*]." Participating in these kinds of ethical dialogues had a transformative effect on my bodily constitution. It made me less anxious about the future and gave me a feeling of confidence and insouciance. The rules of the game change with circumstances such as the occurrence of Ramadan, however.

The Transformation of Interactions during Ramadan

The Ramadan fast is part of a collective ethical practice affecting individuals and the community. Fasting should allow people to experience scarcity and to "feel what it is like to be poor." After having been encouraged to join the fasting by neighbors and friends, I decided to fast for at least the first half of the holy month. I had a last meal every morning around three o'clock and did not eat or drink anything until around eight o'clock in the evening. At the beginning of the month, many people who work during the fast are in a terrible mood—mostly because they have to refrain from smoking. The Ramadan of 2014 (1435 in the Islamic calendar) fell into the hot summer season, when the days are longer and thirst is felt more sharply. In such circumstances, fasting is a confrontation with the self. People told me that it would burn away destructive forms of behavior in a process of spiritual cleansing. While fasting, I often became very emotional. My sensual perception of light and materials such as bed linens and stone surfaces became more intense.

The holy month in Nablus transformed social interactions, and the everyday lateral disciplining grew more explicit. Many Muslims in Nablus praised Christians for either joining the fast or refraining from consuming any water or food in public before the daily breaking of the fast after sunset. These words of praise, I suspected, served as a kind reminder and sometimes had a disciplinary intent. While my interlocutors insisted that fasting is ultimately a matter of individual worship concerning each person in relation to God, many people exercised lateral disciplining by encouraging others to stick to fasting. In the streets, strangers continued to ask me, "Are you fasting?" I usually answered, "Praise be to God [*al-ḥamdu li-llah*]." To this, people generally responded, "May God accept [*allah yataqabbal*]." This phrase means that God may receive and accept one's fasting on the "balance sheet of one's good deeds" (*mīzāniyat al-ḥasanāt*). Another frequent greeting marking the holy month was "May Ramadan be generous [*karīm*]." The response to this was "God is the most generous [*allahu akram*]!"⁹

Many people claimed that they can read in other people's demeanor whether they are genuinely fasting. People therefore avoided displaying any sign of the consumption of liquids or food in public. Once, I walked around holding a bag from which the neck of a newly bought bottle of soda stuck out. This solicited critical comments from people who assumed that I was not fasting and did not even feel ashamed to be drinking in public. I felt compelled to show that I had not yet opened the bottle in my bag. The avoidance of public consumption became even more apparent after I stopped fasting in the middle of Ramadan. I then discovered several hidden places in the backs of shops and in the corners of fruit markets behind wooden counters where small groups of men met during the daytime to share falafel, cigarettes, and tea. Such secret consumption created a different feeling of sociality and encouraged generous sharing in parallel with the pious sharing of food and the generous leniency toward those in need that distinguishes Ramadan from the other months of the year.

While people expected me to hide purchased commodities in nontransparent bags, nobody saw anything wrong with displaying bottles of soda or juice for sale in the market. For a few days, I helped a friend sell bottles of juice. He gave me a water sprinkler so I could make sure there were always little drops of fresh water on the bottles, increasing their seductive appeal in the eyes of the thirsty people passing in the street. Moreover, I was told to build a pyramid with the boxes in which the juice bottles had been delivered and to put single bottles on top. On the first day, I sold off the top of such a pyramid. When my friend saw this, he reprimanded me and asked that I immediately recreate the pyramid, as "this way, the bottles appear to be more." He seemed eager to present his goods in an aesthetic of abundance, which stood in contrast to the generalized call to experience scarcity through fasting.

All of this changed after sunset. In the evenings of early Ramadan, the streets were deserted as people returned home for the daily breaking of the fast. After the first evening meal, the cafés and the streets would fill again with people. Many men spent the entire night outside. Toward the end of Ramadan, more and more men broke their fast in the streets, gathering in small groups around food. Such feasts in public never occurred during the regular days of the year—an indication of how the holy month transforms the ethical regime of visibility. Before breaking the fast, groups of men often gathered around large metal plates filled with meat and rice. This took place in a park, in the street, or in front of a shop in one of the alleys of the market. After the evening prayer, which marked the appropriate moment of breaking the fast, they made sure that everybody near them was also eating. On two occasions, men getting ready to eat saw me passing at a distant corner. Both times, they sent somebody over asking me with both kindness and determination to join their feast. The visibility of open feasts in the streets required participants to invite everyone within view.

The Transformation of Interactions in the Shadow of War

Violence escalating into war further affected interactions during my fieldwork. During the course of Ramadan, which had started at the end of June, the tensions between Israelis and Palestinians escalated. Early in the year, Palestinian political prisoners in Israel had gone on hunger strike. Then, Palestinians abducted three Israeli teenagers from a bus stop near an Israeli settlement next to Hebron and killed them. Spiraling violence ensued. The Israeli military ran arrest operations in the West Bank, killing several Palestinians. Demonstrating Palestinians started clashing regularly with Israeli soldiers. The military wing of Hamas started shooting long-range rockets from Gaza into Israel. Soon thereafter, Israel launched a ground operation against the Gaza Strip lasting from July 8 to August 26, 2014. Since roughly 2007, Israel had imposed a military blockade against the Gaza Strip, limiting the goods that they allowed entry (for a legal definition of this blockade, see United Nations 2009, 16). In response to this, Hamas and other armed groups in the Gaza Strip repeatedly shot rockets into Israel. Some of these rockets were produced locally, while others were smuggled through a system of underground tunnels between the Gaza Strip and Egypt (see Pelham 2014). In reaction to the rocket fire, Israel led several military campaigns against the coastal strip, with violent confrontations taking place in 2008–2009 and 2012. The deadliest recent clash between the Gaza Strip and Israel, however, occurred during my fieldwork in summer 2014—with repercussions in Nablus.

In Nablus, young men regularly marched toward the Israeli checkpoints at the eastern entry to the city, where they got into street fights with Israeli soldiers. At night, the Israeli army took up regular patrolling inside the city of Nablus and conducted arrest operations. My neighbors told me how soldiers stormed into their private homes and destroyed furniture. This climate prevented the markets of Nablus from staying open through the night and, therefore, hindered people from celebrating Ramadan as expected.

As the number of people killed or wounded in the Gaza Strip kept rising throughout the month of Ramadan, people in Nablus began collecting food and clothes to send to the people in the Gaza Strip whose homes had been destroyed by Israeli air raids and shelling. In Nablus, the news of the many civilians killed or wounded and the general destruction in the Gaza Strip overshadowed the three days of celebration at the end of Ramadan. As a sign of mourning, many families refrained from the habitual serving of food or sweets to visiting guests. Families confined themselves to offering black coffee without sugar, similar to the offerings during the mourning surrounding funerals. Israeli army patrols at night prevented shops from staying open and benefiting from people's eagerness to consume more during the holy month.

My fieldwork experiences during Ramadan revealed that there is a shifting consensus on how things should appear in public. I could not find people openly criticizing the consensus, even if many said to me privately that they were not happy about the implicit and explicit disciplining exercised regarding the fast. This suggests that people are under considerable pressure to comply with the requirements for decency in the public sphere. The remaining chapters of this book analyze how people's face-to-face interactions cultivate and sustain different displays of enforcing public decency.

The Ethics of Writing

The heightened sensitivity to how things appear in public creates issues for writing ethnography.[10] To protect pious and honorable reputations, people in contemporary Nablus carefully conceal certain actions, from consuming alcohol to covering the needs of relatives. Respectful ethnographers should avoid exposing their interlocutors in ways that could harm their reputations. At the same time, the richness of the material lies precisely in this back-and-forth between revealing and concealing that distinguishes ethical life. These concerns are nothing new for people writing about Arabic-speaking contexts. In the preface to his famous treatise on the art and practice of love, the great Muslim scholar Ibn Hazm (AD 994–1064) asks God to preserve him and his readers from bewilderment before explicitly addressing the need for anonymizing his informants:

> I must... relate... [my material] as I have personally witnessed, or what I have discovered by diligent research, or matters communicated to me by reliable informants of my own times. Pray excuse me if I sometimes do no more than hint at the names of the heroes, of my anecdotes, and do not mention them more explicitly; this is due either to some shame which I do not hold it permissible to uncover, or in order to protect a loving friend or an illustrious man. It will suffice me to name only those the naming of whom does no harm. (Hazm [1022] 1953, 17)

In writing down my observations, I largely decided to stick to direct interactions between people and the reflections on such interactions that people shared with me. With the exception of publicly known personalities, I refrain from providing personalized portraits of my interlocutors to protect their anonymity. One of the reasons for this is that I do not want to expose them in any indecent way. Another one is the shadow cast by Israeli security surveillance and its collection of personalized and intimate information used to put pressure on Palestinians.

Finally, I decided to include Islamic concepts such as divine provision and divine bookkeeping as theoretical models to help me organize my ethnographic material. In spite of my openness to engaging with Islamic concepts, I had difficulty relating to the work of contemporary Islamic scholars in Palestine. I use empirical social research to understand human practice, whereas many contemporary Islamic scholars give precedence to the text and write studies that focus on concepts and dogmatic reasoning. This has not always been the case; writers such as al-Jahiz (born AD 776), for instance, used empirical methods and what resembles ethnographic writing to discuss issues such as avarice in ninth-century Iraq. Whether the empirical study of ethics, as currently developed within anthropology, will be able to enter into conversation with scholars writing in the Islamic tradition remains an open question.[11] I think that such a project could succeed, if the contemporary Islamic traditions open themselves up to more sociological inquiries. This would allow for comparative studies of lateral disciplining, for instance, across different Islamic and non-Islamic social contexts in the contemporary world. Anthropologists and Islamic scholars could develop a critical perspective for the study of various ways and styles of lateral disciplining, which in the Islamic tradition is discussed under the duty to *command right and forbid wrong* (for an overview, see Cook 2001), in different religious or nonreligious social contexts.

Throughout my time in the field, I took to heart Frantz Fanon's ([1952] 2008, 179) words that there "is no white world, there is no white ethic, any more than there is a white intelligence. There are in every part of the world people who search." Following this injunction, I have attempted to conduct research and to write from a position of respect and openness to different perspectives in the interest of having a scientific conversation on the topics of service provision, mutual aid, and giving under conditions of armed conflict and political repression.

2

Zakat Institutions on Shifting Grounds

Ahmed Sharaf's cell phone kept ringing as he sat down with me to have a conversation about the evolution of institutionalized zakat in the Palestinian territories.[1] It was a winter day in early 2014. Sharaf had recently become the leading *'ālim* (religious scholar, also referred to as *sheikh*) on the Nablus Zakat Committee (NZC). Having just arrived at his office at the local administration office of the Palestinian Authority's Ministry of Religious Affairs, he had not taken off his coat. He excused himself and picked up the phone. The man on the other line wanted to know his opinion regarding a conflict over money. The sheikh listened patiently and promised to meet with the man and the other party to the conflict on Friday to settle the matter. Sharaf tried to calm the man down and said that, given what he had heard so far, the man seemed to be in the right from a "sharia point of view." He reiterated, however, that he would need to speak to the other party as well to arrive at a final opinion. The man on the other line would not stop talking and continued to explain all the things that had happened. Every now and then, the sheikh gave me an apologetic look. On the phone, he remained polite and understanding. When the man finally hung up, Sharaf sighed and said, "This work can be very tiresome. People are calling me all the time, and they want immediate responses. They are simple, here. You cannot tell them to wait and explain to them that you are busy now.... Sometimes, all this gets to be too much. The other day a man told me on the phone that I am not serving him but that he is serving me. At this point, I hung up." The man on the other end of the line seemed to suggest that he had a certain leverage over the sheikh. This is because, in Nablus, any interaction might turn into a story told in the streets, potentially improving or tainting somebody's reputation.

Gossip allows inhabitants of the city to hold other residents and people in positions of authority collectively accountable, at least to a certain degree. Members of zakat committees, for instance, need to manage and cultivate a good reputation lest they lose the trust of the community and, consequently, the ability to attract donations and carry out their work. In interactions with others, therefore, they are laterally disciplined in the sense that they are obliged to present themselves in a good light. As we shall explore in this chapter, they must be responsive to needs, display piety and Islamic virtues, and constantly prove their reliability and efficiency in dealing with zakat funds.

Accountability through local reputation plays a particularly important role in contexts, such as the West Bank and the Gaza Strip, that have been under military rule for more than fifty years. It comes as no surprise that many people see in local gossip a suitable avenue for holding people accountable. This chapter explores the historical development of the NZC since its establishment in 1977 and discusses how accountability through local reputation management does not always align with the administrative tools that government authorities (and their intelligence services) employ for monitoring zakat institutions—tools that have long been seen as illegitimate, repressive, and detached from local realities. For this purpose, I draw on leaflets and legal documents, as well as interviews with former NZC members. While many institutions, such as the NZC, bear *zakat* in their name, they also collect and distribute donations of sadaqa. In the following, *zakat* will be used in a generic sense to speak about Islamic pious gifts of movable wealth.

After the Palestinian Authority forcefully closed more than ninety zakat committees across the West Bank in 2007 and replaced them with roughly a dozen committees under its direct political control, these institutions lost the trust of local communities and became dysfunctional. During my fieldwork in 2013 and 2014, however, a new zakat committee composed of politically independent personalities, such as Ahmed Sharaf, sought to regain the trust of the population by cultivating a reputation for financial integrity and Islamic piety. To illustrate this aspect of the NZC's history, I draw on my own ethnographic material to describe how these new members sought to improve the reputation of the NZC in their everyday interactions with people from the community and thereby made themselves accountable to them.

The Historical Development of Institutionalized Zakat in Nablus

Twentieth-century Palestinians witnessed the emergence of institutions collecting and distributing zakat in a legal framework. It is not necessary for zakat funds to flow through institutions: they can also change hands during face-to-face encounters between givers and recipients. Interpreters of the Quran, however, have long considered the pooling of zakat funds by intermediaries arranging their distribution as legitimate on the basis of the Quran (9, 60, discussed in the introduction). The idea of creating committees that pool zakat and arrange for its distribution has been firmly retained in the Islamic scholarly tradition (on which, see, for example, the work of Ghazali [(1097) 1966, 23–25], who lived in the eleventh century). The zakat institutions established in Palestine in the twentieth century see themselves in alignment with such long-standing traditions. Since the 1970s, the NZC has become regionally known for its effective work, strong local roots, and compliance with a legal framework defined by the state of Jordan. However, the institutionalization of zakat started earlier.

In 1907, shortly before the fall of the Ottoman Empire in 1917, institutions collecting and distributing zakat in Palestine were registered by Ottoman rulers in a newly crafted legal framework allowing them to exercise governmental control over the flow of zakat funds.[2] Previously, the regulation of charitable giving during the Ottoman era mainly focused on endowments (*waqf*) of immovable property rather than on zakat funds (Singer 2018, 10). According to Fahmi Ansari, a librarian in East Jerusalem whom I interviewed in 2014, Islamic authorities in Ottoman Istanbul had no connection to zakat collection in Palestine. Ansari claimed that the general population (*'awām*) in Ottoman Palestine collected and distributed zakat as a form of worship, so such interactions occurred outside the administrative influence of the government. According to Moumtaz (2021, 157–169), zakat and sadaqa practices in the Ottoman Empire before the modernist reforms of the later nineteenth century largely focused on caring for the family and close kin.[3]

In Nablus, official structures for pooling zakat emerged as early as 1956, when the Jordanian government registered the Tadamun Islamic Charitable Society, allowing a group of men from important families to teach Quran memorization and sharia, to provide informal justice consultations, and to offer aid to people in need.[4] When Israel occupied the West Bank in 1967, the Jordanian government continued administering the civil affairs of the Palestinian population, including zakat. In 1977, the Jordanian government registered the NZC as the first institution of its kind in the entire region. It granted legal status to a hitherto informal group of men who had been collecting and distributing zakat from within the Hanbali Mosque in the old city of Nablus.[5] Legal registration granted the members of the NZC access to international funding, resulting in a gradual diversification of charitable activities. Over the years, the NZC became seen as an exemplary model of effective zakat, and its projects were partly replicated in other cities of the West Bank (Schaeublin, 2009), Jerusalem (Iwais and Schaeublin 2011), the Gaza Strip (Schaeublin 2012), and Jordan (Clark 2004, 109–110, 153).

In 1988, Jordanian administrators governing the civil affairs of Palestinians living under Israeli military rule formalized the zakat committee model in the Jordanian Zakat Fund Law Number 8 of the Year 1988. According to this law, a central zakat fund within Jordan's government was the only body entitled to establish and supervise zakat committees in different parts of Jordan and the West Bank. The zakat committees in cities and towns were locally autonomous in their operations and effectively had a monopoly on the collection and distribution of zakat funds. Receiving zakat from donors inside and outside the country, the committees were obliged to pay 10 to 20 percent of their annual income to the central Zakat Fund.

Within this legal framework, the NZC developed institutional relations with donor organizations in the United Arab Emirates, Kuwait, Saudi Arabia, Qatar, the United States, the United Kingdom, Jordan, France, and Canada (Nablus Zakat Committee [2000–2004?], 2). The Palestinian zakat committees in the 1990s were financially independent from the Palestinian Authority, as well as from European and American governmental and nongovernmental organizations. Not being "docile" to such donor apparatuses allowed them to determine their own priorities and to develop projects in accordance with local communities (Hilal and Maliki 1997, 62).

Until the NZC was forcefully taken over by the Palestinian Authority in 2008, a considerable degree (up to 90%) of local funding further enhanced its autonomy.[6] An important source of income for the NZC is its *waqf* properties. *Waqf* is technically a subcategory of sadaqa because it generates a regular stream of wealth or services that benefits the community (Hallaq 2009, 142–146). In Islamic history, *waqf* endowments led to the building of "mosques, Sufi *khanqahs*, hospitals, public fountains, soup kitchens, traveler's lodges, and a variety of public works, notably bridges. . . . A typical waqf consisted of a mosque and rental property (e.g., shops), the rent from which supported the operation and maintenance of the mosque" (Hallaq 2009, 142).[7] Since its inception, the NZC had developed a plot of *waqf* land of fifty thousand square meters on the northern hill—bought with donations and investments by the committee.[8] On this land, the committee built a hospital and rented the building out to the University of Nablus. The income from the rent goes to the zakat committee, constituting a constant flow of sadaqa. On the rest of the *waqf* plot, the committee built a middle school and an elementary school for orphans. Over the years, the committee developed its activities and projects, including social work monitoring families in need, regular financial support, emergency aid to families, in-kind aid, animals for slaughter for religious feasts, orphan sponsorship programs, scholarships, financial aid for medical treatments, Quran memorization centers, and a medical complex attached to a mosque (Nablus Zakat Committee [2000–2004?], 8–12). The committee also established a dairy, which was the first Palestinian factory in the West Bank producing pasteurized milk—and hence a step toward independence from Israeli agriculture.[9]

After the Oslo peace agreement between Israel and the Palestinian Liberation Organization in 1993, Yassir Arafat, presiding over the newly established Palestinian Authority, made the Jordanian zakat committee model one of his tools of governance.[10] In the period after Oslo, the Palestinian territories witnessed a proliferation of secular NGOs funded by North American and European governments. In this context, "zakat committees enjoy[ed] a tremendous amount of legitimacy. Even secular leftists admire[d] their authenticity and ability to operate without reliance on Western funding" (Brown 2003, 160). The Jordanian zakat laws remained applicable in the West Bank, as Arafat relegated the drafting of a Palestinian zakat law to the final establishment of Palestinian statehood.[11] Arafat defined the Palestinian Authority's Ministry of Awqaf and Religious Affairs along the lines of its Jordanian equivalent and placed the *waqf* lands, Islamic affairs, and zakat committees in the West Bank and the Gaza Strip under its responsibility. The zakat committees formally became part of the Palestinian Authority—even if they retained their local autonomy. However, Palestinian intelligence services kept zakat committees and their members under tight scrutiny after 1996, as they knew that the loyalty of local zakat committees could swing toward the political forces opposing the Palestinian Authority (Schaeublin 2009, 59).

Since the 2000s, the Israeli and US governments have been voicing concerns about alleged links between the Palestinian zakat committees and Hamas. After the Hamas-led Change and Reform bloc won municipal and parliamentary elections in 2005 and 2006, the question arose whether the committee contributed directly to Hamas's popularity among Palestinian voters. In its electoral campaign, Hamas tried to monopolize Islamic symbols and images, while promising constructive policies and political measures against corruption (Hroub 2006). A number of secularists argued that Hamas benefited from zakat committees' Islamic appearance and reputation for financial integrity. Internal Palestinian tensions degenerated into armed clashes between Hamas and Fatah. When Hamas took control of the Gaza Strip by force in 2007, a Fatah-dominated emergency cabinet backed by Israel and the United States sought to control the West Bank and decided to bring the zakat sector in there under its direct political control.

In the West Bank, more than ninety committees were shut down and replaced by eleven new central committees under the control of the Palestinian Authority. Being situated in one of the major cities of the West Bank, the NZC was first closed and then forced to hand over its properties and funds to a committee newly composed of people known for their loyalty to the Palestinian Authority. The NZC was thus transformed into one of the new central committees. In hindsight, the closures of zakat committees in the West Bank appear to have occurred under pressure from the Israeli and US governments (Milton-Edwards 2017; see also Wikileaks 2008). To justify these heavy-handed interferences in the zakat sector, the Palestinian Authority argued that zakat committees were fronts for Hamas, in spite of diverging opinions emphasizing the political pluralism of these institutions.[12] This led to a new authoritarianism in the field of zakat, which also had repercussions in the Gaza Strip, where Hamas increased government control over zakat institutions. Palestinian zakat institutions continued to entertain intimate links with security forces. In the Gaza Strip, police officers of the Hamas-led government there started serving as committee members (Schaeublin 2012, 69–70). In the West Bank, the zakat committees started to work more closely with security forces.

In the aftermath of the 2007 reorganization of the zakat sector in the West Bank, the new zakat committees lacked funding, and projects such as medical clinics and the dairy in Nablus became dysfunctional. Popular confidence in the committees waned.[13] In 2011, the annual turnover of zakat committees in the West Bank was down to an estimated 20 percent compared to pre-2007.[14] At that time, the Palestinian Authority realized that centralization in the field of zakat was not working because the damage to the local legitimacy of the zakat committees was too drastic. Accordingly, the Palestinian Authority issued decrees allowing for the reopening of local subcommittees under the supervision of the central committees. The new NZC, as one of the central committees, thus started overseeing subcommittees in the adjacent villages.

In the years after 2007, the members of the NZC appointed by the Palestinian Authority remained unable to run activities and resigned in 2010 (Maan News 2010). However, it took until 2013 for a new committee to be appointed that was mainly made up of personalities known for a certain independence from the continued Hamas and Fatah division running through Palestinian politics (*Raya News Agency* 2013). This new NZC, along with other such arrangements in committees across the West Bank, was relatively successful. By 2019, the number of zakat committees in the West Bank had increased to forty-one, according to an employee of the Palestinian Authority's Ministry of Awqaf.

Rendering Zakat Collection and Distribution Systematic

Legal formalization went along with the development of administrative tools used by the NZC to render the distribution of zakat funds more systematic. Adly Yaish actively shaped the NZC as a member until 2005, when he was elected mayor of Nablus and resigned from the committee. He is a locally respected personality and businessman with a good reputation who sells Mercedes cars. People have referred to him as an exemplar of honesty and transparency. Even his political enemies sometimes told me that Hajj (a title for people who have been on the pilgrimage to Mecca) Adly is "gold"—highlighting his integrity in dealing with others. Yaish told me in 2013 that, when he was still a boy, his father used to take him to the old city, where most of the poor households in Nablus were located. They went to different shopkeepers and asked them which families in the neighborhood were short of money. Shopkeepers knew these things because they observed the consumption patterns of people in the neighborhood. On the basis of the hints given at the shops, Yaish and his father visited families in their homes. According to Yaish, mosques also pooled knowledge about the people in the vicinity. Men running mosques sent people out to look for deprived households and made sure to cover their needs.

Once the NZC was established in 1977, Yaish's father and the other members scaled up this more systematic (*niẓāmī*) approach to zakat. They conducted surveys on poor households and identified two hundred families. To their surprise, they discovered that a number of them were receiving zakat from different donors, while others only from a few. This imbalance pushed them to improve the coordination of zakat. To prevent certain families from deceiving their donors, they started keeping detailed records on the recipients. Resorting to surveys and statistics, they generated what Adly Yaish called "clean knowledge." According to him, this helped them gain the trust of people in Nablus, who started confiding their zakat to the committee.

Abd al-Rahim al-Hanbali is a veterinarian known for his Islamic literacy who long served as president of the NZC and was forced to resign in 2007. People in Nablus treated Hanbali with reverence, often coming out of their shops to kiss his cheeks and greet him warmly when he passed by. They considered him a sheikh, a pious man to whom one could turn for ethical guidance. He advised people on how to cope with marital and other kinds of relational problems. In his conversations with others in the streets of Nablus, he ceaselessly cited the Quran and the sayings of Prophet Mohammed. Hanbali succeeded his father as president of the NZC and played a key role in setting up the zakat committee's dairy (Benthall 2008, 15). He was involved in the zakat committee for several decades until 2007, when he was obliged to hand the committee over to the new one appointed by the Palestinian Authority. During an interview in 2013, Hanbali told me that a "systematic" approach serves to preserve the dignity of destitute families by transmitting "zakat to the poor via bank accounts [avoiding the recipients being seen by their neighbors when receiving money]." Moreover, he mentioned the committee's efforts to establish a system of keeping and updating files on families on the basis of social visits and inquiries in the neighborhood carried out by both male and female staff to gain a complete picture.

Gradually, the NZC introduced new techniques of administration to keep track of individuals and nuclear families with a view to their material situation and their ways of living. The self-description of the Nablus Zakat Committee (1998) states that the committee "follows up on poor families and orphans religiously, educationally, economically, medically, and socially." This overarching goal is explicitly emphasized in the same document: "The committee aims at linking [rabṭ] people to God, Exalted and Sublime, spreading religious consciousness [al-waʿī al-dīnī], and inculcating the true [ṣaḥīḥa] Islamic conviction [ʿaqīda] in the selves [nufūs] of the sons of the Islamic community [ummah]. This is achieved through the spreading of Quran memorization centers in the region and their supervision [through the committee]."

At the time of my fieldwork in 2013 and 2014, the social workers of the NZC seemed little concerned with the convictions of people in need and stated that Christians are also eligible for aid from the committee. Perhaps the emphasis on religious conviction was mitigated after the forced closures in 2007. In any case, the main job of the social workers lay in generating and regularly updating reliable knowledge on poor households in Nablus. They inferred the financial needs of a household from a family's behavior. For this purpose, they drew on statements by people within the neighborhoods and their observations of members of poor households.

Three female and two male social workers regularly visited families and kept files on all recipients of zakat or sadaqa disbursed through the committee. A woman who had been in that job for twenty-six years described her work as this:

> We go to the heart of the household [qalb al-dār] and then write down all the information we need on the family in order to fill out the file. Then, we ask the family whom in the neighborhood they would like us to question about them. We [merely make sure to assess the need of the family and] do

not ask about debts and do not get involved in tensions between the poor family and others. Oftentimes, we go to talk to the head of the neighborhood [*mukhtār al-ḥāra*], who then leads us to hidden [i.e., poor] families [concealing their financial needs from others].[15]

This bureaucratic formalization of zakat distribution within the committees helped to bring all forms of zakat transfers passing through institutional bodies under the oversight of the state by means of reporting tools, as stipulated by the Jordanian zakat law.[16] Keeping files and producing financial reports for governmental oversight bodies has been part of the general push toward making zakat practice systematic. When the Palestinian Authority took over the NZC in 2008, all the documents, bank accounts, and properties that the old committee handed over were reportedly flawless (Palestinian Authority Ministry of Awqaf 2008).

Zakat Committees as Perceived Security Threat

In spite of this bureaucratization of zakat, the zakat sector in the West Bank started to be perceived as a security threat in the 2000s, giving rise to new forms of surveillance of zakat flows through the committees. In this context, the Palestinian zakat committees faced allegations of channeling funds to Hamas's military or political activities. There are, in fact, indications that zakat funds could be used to support Palestinian resistance. While the Jordanian law partly took up the categories of eligible beneficiaries as laid out in the Quran (listed in the introduction), it also mentions "the activists [or fighters] on God's path [*al-mujāhidīn fī sabīl allah*]" as possible beneficiaries of zakat.[17] This wording appears to echo the expression "in the way of God," listed in the Quran. The use of the term *mujāhidīn* (fighters or activists) operating "in the way of God" raises the question of whether zakat and sadaqa can be used for military projects, such as the armed resistance against Israeli military occupation. In 1968, the grand mufti of Saudi Arabia issued a recommendation declaring the use of zakat for supporting Palestinian resistance legitimate (Hegghammer 2010, 20). This authorization, however, was conditional on the Saudi government supervising expenditures.

The use of the expression "in the way of God" in the Jordanian zakat law could be explained by the historical context of the 1980s and early 1990s, when the terms *mujāhidīn* and *jihad* were not yet viewed with the same suspicion by Western policy circles as in the aftermath of the 9/11 attacks. In the 1980s, when the Jordanian zakat law was drafted, the US government actively supported Afghan *mujāhidīn* confronting the Soviet invasion (Benthall 2021). Moreover, the expression "in the way of God" as one of the eight legitimate categories for spending zakat is contested among Muslim scholars (Benthall and Bellion-Jourdan 2009, 69–84; Kuran 2003) because of its ambiguous meaning spanning efforts of a military, educational, and moral nature.[18]

In spite of this ambiguity, no court has so far convicted West Bank zakat committees of misusing or diverting funds, and studies suggest that the committees included different political movements (even leftist groups) and not only people known for their proximity to Hamas.[19] With the available evidence, the question of whether Palestinian zakat committees ever channeled funding directly supporting armed struggle cannot be answered conclusively. Families of Palestinian martyrs and political prisoners in Israel have received support from zakat committees. However, it seems that the committees did not treat them differently than they did families who had lost their breadwinners for reasons unrelated to the Palestinian struggle against Israeli occupation (for a detailed discussion of this topic, see Benthall 2017).

The question as to whether and how Hamas did control the zakat committees in the West Bank before 2007 proved to have more severe legal implications. Since the early 2000s, the US government has created a legal landscape for criminalizing any direct or indirect "material support" to a designated terrorist organization (for a general discussion, see James 2019a). The broad definition of "material support" as adopted by the US Supreme Court makes international Islamic donors and banks working with Palestinian zakat committees a possible target for lawsuits, if the plaintiffs can produce any proof suggesting that the work of the zakat committees in any way benefited Hamas.

This transformation of the legal landscape in the United States had incisive consequences for the zakat committees and the international institutions working with them. In US courts, it became possible to argue that the zakat committees were serving the interests of Hamas by enhancing the movement's political agenda through "winning [the] hearts and minds" of the Palestinian population. Against this background, any institution that had provided financial support or financial services (such as wiring bank transfers) to Palestinian zakat committees could be held liable for "supporting terrorism"—leading to a series of legal proceedings, mainly in the United States and Europe (see Benthall 2011a, 2011b, 2016, 2017).

The drastic drop of turnover in the NZC and other West Bank zakat committees after 2007 partly results from the chilling effect on donations of such allegations of proximity to terrorism (see James 2019b). Another factor is that the former donors—both local and international—did not trust the new committees composed in 2008 and refused to work with them, notably because they felt that they were now too close to the notorious corruption and cronyism of the Palestinian Authority. The gap in aid provision resulting from the faltering of zakat committees was partly filled by an increase in the European Commission's social welfare funding channeled through the Palestinian Authority's Ministry of Social Affairs (Schaeublin 2012, 80). The European Commission was running all the names of beneficiaries through a digital list of terror suspects maintained by World-Check, a private security company originating in South Africa.[20]

The proliferation of such security databases gradually forced transnational donors under increasing pressure to provide extremely detailed documentation on their expenditures to fend off possible accusations of supporting terrorism. Due diligence to prevent zakat or sadaqa funds reaching "terrorists" led to the widespread vetting of recipients against various terror lists (Bhungalia 2015, 2315; de Goede 2012; James 2019a; Kocher 2011). The trend of governing zakat practice as a security issue is palpable in the NZC's everyday practices. During my fieldwork, I often witnessed how the zakat committee distributed aid coming from different international Islamic charities, based in such countries as the United Kingdom, Turkey, or Saudi Arabia. People on the beneficiary lists of the zakat committee were called up and invited to pass by the committee's premises to pick up food parcels or financial aid distributed on behalf of donors abroad. At times, the international donor institution was asking the zakat committees to put up a poster with their logo during the distribution and to take pictures of every beneficiary receiving aid. Apparently, many donor institutions insisted on such procedures to account for every penny they spent to the intelligence apparatuses in the country in which they were based.

According to rumors, donor organizations working with zakat committees started vetting lists of beneficiaries with the help of terror databases run by private security companies (see, e.g., James 2019b, 156–157). Taking pictures of recipients and running their names through such databases, however, runs counter to the need to protect the dignity of recipients through discretion, which is a prominent aspect of zakat in the Islamic tradition (Schaeublin 2019). Consequently, the use of security databases is extremely delicate and difficult to research. Zakat institutions are hesitant to share information on the issue because they are in sort of a double bind. If they say that they do use antiterrorist vetting procedures, they may damage their respectability in local communities, which see these lists as illegitimate tools of control. On the other hand, if they publicly state that they do not resort to vetting procedures, they risk being accused of a lack of due diligence and compliance with international security policies.

This illustrates the tricky situation that zakat committees working under Israeli military rule find themselves in. They are held accountable by local governments, international security apparatuses, and international lawsuits against their donors and banks. At the same time, they are held accountable by the local community, whose gossiping determines whether committee members succeed in maintaining a good reputation, which is indispensable to the task of pooling and distributing zakat funds.

Local Accountability through Reputation

Reputation is key to how zakat committees are constituted. The Jordanian zakat law explicitly refers to this when defining the criteria for the composition of these committees. The 1996 Regulations (Article 4) list the following conditions for becoming a member of a zakat committee:

1. To be of Jordanian [respectively, Palestinian] nationality;
2. To be of good conduct [*sīra*], demeanor [*sulūk*], and reputation and not to be convicted of a felony or any misdemeanor in violation of honor [*sharaf*] or general morals [*akhlāq 'āmma*];
3. To be descendants [from families from] the governorate, district, or region [where] the committee works;
4. And to be literate.

The emphasis on reputation, conduct, demeanor, honor, and morals as key qualities suggests that zakat committee members must be known within the communities they work in. These principles seem to have rubbed off on the public perception of zakat committees more generally. Before 2007, they had a reputation for financial integrity (in contrast to the Palestinian Authority) and for a commitment to Islamic ethics. Their board members tended to be locally rooted and representative of different political colors. Moreover, the Jordanian zakat law actively prevents a specific family or tribe from taking control of the committee and stipulates in its 1996 Regulations (Article 3d) that no relatives up to the fourth degree are to be represented in the same zakat committee. Finally, people repeatedly emphasized that zakat committee members need to know about the economy, (financial) management, and religion. This is why committees often include small and medium-sized entrepreneurs, personalities known for their Islamic literacy, and people involved in local politics.

Men compose most zakat committees in Palestine. However, there are exceptions of women on many committees, including the one in Nablus. In general, however, women are more active as employees and social workers of zakat committees and also often play a key role in ensuring the discretion of zakat transfers to protect the dignity of recipients (see chap. 4).

An employee of the Palestinian Authority overseeing zakat committees across the West Bank told me that, since 2013, it has become more common for women to be represented on zakat committees. At the same time, she insisted that concerns with reputation continued to play a major role for building and maintaining popular confidence in the committees.[21] Her advice to new committee members was to be modest, honest, close to the people, respectable, distant from any tensions arising from family honor, direct and open in asking wealthy people for money, and free of any tattoos.

After the Palestinian Authority's takeover of the NZC in 2007 and the falling apart of the Fatah loyalists replacing the old guard, new committee members tried to regain popular confidence. This process was ongoing during my fieldwork. The new committee members sought to prove their ability to effectively and responsibly deal with zakat funds. Aware of the likelihood that their success would depend on the community's level of trust in them, they sought to build up a good reputation. In this endeavor, they seemed extremely mindful of how they presented themselves in public interactions.

Public Interactions as Ethical Observatory

Ahmed Sharaf, who is mentioned in the vignette at the beginning of this chapter, was among these new members of the NZC seeking to rebuild trust. He had been the imam of the Great Mosque in Nablus and established himself as a popular and trusted person in the city. Long before joining the zakat committee, he had already been under the observation of the local community. One day in 2014, I was discussing with a librarian whether the new zakat committee members could be trusted. She said that some of them were exemplars of good conduct. She told me that she had already observed Ahmed Sharaf when he came to a library to study for a degree from the Sharia Faculty of the University of Nablus: "He was very conscientious and meticulous in his way of studying. In my eyes, he has the qualities [*ṣifāt*] of the Prophet, such as truthfulness [*ṣidq*], trustworthiness [*amāna*], and fairness [*nazāha*]. This is not self-evident for people working in mosques as employees of the Palestinian Authority's Ministry of Awqaf where not everybody has good ethical conduct [*akhlāq*]. His conduct, however, is exceptional."

When I met him in meetings and interactions with others, Sharaf seemed always aware that his behavior was under public scrutiny. Together with other members of the newly composed zakat committee, he often fasted on regular weekdays. I often saw zakat committee members looking tired in the afternoon.

In meetings with others, they calmly refused to drink, explaining that they were fasting. Their gestures and their facial expressions manifested pious self-restraint and modesty.

Abu Faruk, a local entrepreneur who had joined the zakat committee in 2014, continually lent his ear to people when going around the city (fig. 2.1). He would often drive around and distribute cooked meals from the city's soup kitchen. Moving in public space, he displayed his reliance on God in all of his undertakings by saying "in the name of God" or "oh Lord" before entering a door or starting a car. For him, distributing food and looking after households in need was intimately tied to his everyday practices as a pious Muslim, such as regularly praying and learning how to properly recite the Quranic text.

The community's observation and ethical judgment of zakat committee members has a regulatory function and creates local accountability. As people are observed and ethically judged in social interactions, it becomes possible for any inhabitant of the city to exercise a kind of lateral disciplining with members of the zakat committee. The latter know that their reputation could be tainted by the people they interact with, as the man in the phone call with Sheikh Ahmed Sharaf seems to imply. In this context, the zakat committee members' display of virtuous signs is not merely about cultivating a pious self (Mahmood 2005) but also about presenting oneself to others. Drawing on Goffman (1959), Keane (2015, 147) has written about this "ethical work" of presenting oneself. The "talk of the town" interpreting and judging people is crucial for a mechanism of accountability that works through people's reputation in an enclosed community. At the time of my fieldwork, zakat committee members seemed highly aware they were being observed and judged by the inhabitants of Nablus. They made sure to display virtues such as patience, modesty, reliance on God, honesty, and fairness—all derived from Islamic scriptures—when interacting with others.

The force of accountability through such lateral disciplining in the ethical observatory becomes obvious when the reputation of the committee members is tainted. This happened, for instance, after 2007 when the Fatah loyalists in the NZC failed to manage their reputation, trust was lost, and the activities of the committee were disrupted. Local donations to the committee stopped, as people started to give most of their zakat and sadaqa directly to people in need. International donors also quickly ceased their transfers to the NZC. People questioned the new members' moral and financial integrity and suspected connections to the corruption of the Palestinian Authority. Between 2008 and 2012, people described the committee as tattered (*muhtari'a*) and flimsy (*mhalhala*)—in stark contrast to the pre-2007 committee, whose members were seen as coming from wealthy families, paying zakat to the committee from

Figure 2.1. Abu Faruk, with a bag of food for a household in need, listening to a man in the old city. © Jonas Opperskalski

their own money, committed to religion, and realizing projects with tangible and visible effects for the community. A moderator from Radio Quran Nablus, whom I interviewed in 2014, told me that the committee composed in 2013 was still struggling to build trust: "The judgment of the new committee depends on people's opinions. People observe the new committee members closely."

This local observation and judgment of zakat committee members seems to enable communities to hold zakat institutions in Palestine to a certain degree locally accountable over the years. For this reason, the Palestinian Authority appears to have returned to delegating the selection of zakat committee members in the West Bank to the local level (Schaeublin 2012, 83).

Torn among the judgment of the community, governmental oversight, Israeli military rule, and international security surveillance and databases used for vetting procedures developed for "combating the financing of terrorism" (Biersteker and Eckert 2008; de Goede 2012), local practitioners of zakat need to be agile to adapt zakat projects in a shifting and politically challenging context. Since 2012, the NZC has been running a soup kitchen with staff and volunteers cooking food and distributing it to poor households.[22] One day in 2014, women from neighboring villages and towns came to Nablus to learn how to set up a similar project in their hometowns. One of the women who had initiated the soup kitchen in Nablus gave them a list of principles to guide their actions:

- When you have people's trust, funding comes to you from local sources.
- Do not rely on international sources, as they may cease anytime.
- Make sure all your employees donate a tiny portion of their salary to the soup kitchen.
- Avoid cooking frozen meat.
- Stay away from those exerting tyrannical power [*jabarūt*] or authoritarianism [*taḥakkum*].
- Arrange for an office of the Palestinian Authority to follow up on your activities—if you would like to walk a straight line [*timshī ṣaḥḥ*].
- Do not make the food-aid conditional. Conditions [*sharṭ*] are not acceptable from a sharia point of view.

This list provides a sense of what it means on a practical level to maneuver different kinds of accountability. Local trust—and local funding as proof of that trust—appears to be the condition sine qua non for running successful zakat projects. The quality of the food distributed as zakat or sadaqa is as important as involving everyone who participates in the project in the act of pious giving (even if it is only a tiny amount). At the same time, one needs to keep clean financial records and make sure that the Palestinian Authority follows up on one's spending, without moving in close proximity to people exercising authoritarian rule—of whom there are many in the Palestinian Authority. On the whole, this kind of agility endows the Palestinian zakat sector with considerable resilience, even in a context of continued military occupation and persistent problems for banks and international donors working with zakat committees.

Between Political Repression and Local Accountability

Pooling funds that spring from Islamic pious giving and arranging their distribution under repressive rule gives rise to a dilemma. If such institutions move too closely to governing structures that people perceive as corrupt and repressive, they no longer receive zakat from the population. On the other hand, if they go too far in evading state control, governments might perceive them as subversive to their rule (at best) or as a channel of funding for potentially "terrorist" militancy (at worst). Against this background, successful zakat institutions in Arab-Muslim-majority countries need to reconcile different demands. They are held accountable by the local communities they serve, (authoritarian) governments, and emerging digital mechanisms of security surveillance in the context of the war on terror, such as global terrorist databases.

Since the 1970s, zakat institutions in many places have evolved in a climate of political repression. The legal frameworks and policies advanced by different governments in states where people practice zakat were marked by a certain suspicion toward Islamic institutions (Pierret and Selvik 2009; De Cordier 2010; Lacey and Benthall 2014; Erie 2016). This is less the case in Jordan. Here, the Muslim Brotherhood constitutes a kind of loyal opposition to the monarchy, and zakat institutions have become an integrated part of the state's welfare system (Clark 2004). In places where state structures remain weak, outsiders tend to perceive zakat institutions as possibly subversive social wings of Islamic political movements such as Hizbullah in Lebanon (Deeb 2006; Cammett 2014). The Palestinian case is specific to the extent that the Palestinian Authority operates under the tutelage of Israeli military rule. Palestinians gradually came to perceive the agency governing them as being complicit in the wider repressive landscape of Israeli occupation. Some of the Palestinian

Authority's branches, however, continue to be seen as constructively supporting Palestinian self-governance and therefore retain a certain legitimacy. In the course of recent history, the Palestinian zakat committees had to navigate these shifting political grounds, confronting Israeli military raids, confiscations, and interferences in their managing boards, while also relying on official support (within limits) to rebuild local trust and continue to provide basic care services.

In spite of the political turmoil created by the Hamas-Fatah division since 2007, zakat giving never ceased. Its quality as both a personal virtue (a pious act of giving) and an obligation legally formalized in changing historical contexts endows it with a considerable malleability (on the plasticity of the Islamic tradition in changing circumstances, see Clarke 2018). When the intermediary institutions coordinating its collection and distribution crumble, givers resort to disbursing their zakat directly to people in need and later return to giving it to an institution they trust. In other words, political interference cannot significantly prevent people from worshipping God through giving. As a result of the Palestinian Authority's repressive intervention in the zakat sector in the West Bank, zakat distributions started flowing in informal and discreet channels beyond the purview of governments that the following chapters discuss in detail. My interlocutors emphasized the malleability of zakat in adapting to adverse circumstances: when institutional channels closed, zakat would simply find other ways to flow.

Zakat committee members' attempts to gain popular confidence highlight the importance of embodying and displaying signs of piety and moral integrity in social interactions in Nablus. The following chapters continue to explore how social interactions in Nablus constitute a field, partly marked by Islamic discourse, wherein people cultivate certain kinds of ethical appearance and discipline one another laterally. The next chapter turns to the ethics of interaction surrounding people in financial distress who are torn between exposing their own need to others in hope of receiving support and the desire to hold on to a dignified and honorable appearance by concealing their material want from others.

3

Concealing and Exposing Need

Shyness, Piety, and Dignity

I often went to the popular Hammouz Café in Nablus to meet friends or warm myself up at the woodstove on cold winter days. A respectable family of the same name has run the café ever since its establishment in 1892. The part of the city where the café is situated, on the slope of the southern hill to the west of the old city, was built in the late nineteenth century. The café's spacious premises belong to the municipality of Nablus. As the café goes back several generations, its current owners pay very little rent. This allows them to offer coffee, tea, lemonade, and tobacco on water pipes at low prices. Rayiq al-Hammouz, the current owner, describes it as follows: "The café is a source of income [*rizq*] and through it you look upon the world.... The café is [an object of] longing for the city [*al-qahwa ḥanīn li-l-balad*]."[1] The café is also a place where men from different social classes would meet. Here, melancholic elderly men owning wealth and real estate would mingle with young workers, students, market traders, and travelers. Occasionally, even a rabbi from the Arabic-speaking Samaritan village on the southern hill would stop by to play a game of backgammon. Very few women would come to the café. When they did, the waiters would serve them like anybody else, but certain men in the café would give them skeptical looks.

One Ramadan night, men recovered from a day's fasting were playing cards and drinking tamarind juice, lemonade, coffee, or tea on the spacious terrace. My friend Abu Walid, a man in his late twenties, and I were playing a game of backgammon at a table shared with two men and the only two women among the guests. An old man appeared. Wearing worn-out clothes, he held a metal plate right above the middle of our table. He was trying to sell pieces of chocolate for a very small price. Abu Walid looked up from the backgammon board and told him in Arabic, "Thank you, but we do not need this. May God give you the force to stand your ground [*allah yajbur 'an-ak*]." The old man kept holding the plate at the level of our heads, implicitly urging others at the table to buy the sweets. No one responded until one of the young men who had been talking to the women threw a five-shekel coin (about one dollar) on his plate and said, "Take this and leave!" After a moment of silence, the sweets seller shouted, "Shameful [*'ayb*]!" He took the five-shekel coin and put it in the middle of our backgammon board on the little bench between the two halves. We stared at the coin, saying nothing, as the old man turned away and moved on through the rows of chairs.

In Nablus, interactions between affluent people and those struck by financial scarcity require a specific kind of tactfulness. Such tact was manifest in Abu Walid's respectful invocation of God's protection as he refused the old man's offer to sell him chocolate. By contrast, when the younger man disdainfully threw a coin without taking a piece of chocolate, it exposed the old man as a beggar. The old man refused to be publicly shamed in such a way. He returned the money and scolded the young man for his inappropriate and insulting behavior. The old man's use of the word *'ayb* was intended to make shame stick to the other party in the interaction. Such public scenes risk giving rise to local gossip and thereby tainting the reputation of both parties involved. The high stakes in such interactions provides those who are in poverty with a certain power to defend their honor, regain the moral high ground, and laterally discipline others for their offenses.

This chapter focuses on how people in situations of acute material need navigate everyday economic interactions, including informal zakat transactions, while retaining their dignity. In the three years prior to my fieldwork (2010 to 2013), Palestinians living in the West Bank had become poorer and their economy had contracted (World Bank 2015, 1). This was also a period during which the Nablus Zakat Committee (NZC) had become largely dysfunctional. In 2014, as the NZC was slowly recovering, unemployment in Nablus was at 21.6 percent and the average daily wage for employees was about $20 (101 Israeli shekels). This was one of the lowest average wages of all West Bank governorates.[2] Since the crackdown against zakat committees in 2007, many people in Nablus increasingly had started paying their zakat and sadaqa directly to neighbors, friends, or relatives in need. While such direct giving has always been an integral part of zakat practice, the fact that people did not yet fully trust the new NZC made informal zakat transfers more widespread than in previous years. This shift to direct giving highlights the malleability of zakat practice in adapting to changing and repressive political conditions.[3] On the other hand, direct giving involves face-to-face interactions between givers and receivers that are delicate to navigate.

People in dire financial straits are extremely sensitive about being perceived as poor. At the same time, they depend on small gifts of money and food, which most people in Nablus explicitly or implicitly understand to be a form of zakat or sadaqa. There are various tactics of concealing such gifts lest they expose the recipients as poor. Generally, both givers and receivers try to conceal explicit material need. In certain situations, however, people selectively reveal their need in an attempt to discipline a more affluent party into giving.

Exposed need challenges not only the dignity of individuals but also the reputations of their families. Such concerns for reputation raise the stakes in the concealing and exposing of material need in Nablus. When someone openly displays need under the public gaze, people describe this as exposing or scandalizing their relatives. My interlocutors consistently referred to openly visible need as *'ayb* (shameful) in the sense of tarnishing the reputation of family members and tainting their honor.[4] Many families thus dwelled in hiding of sorts, surviving on the support of people who were discreetly looking after them. People called giving to such families an act of covering (*satara*), in the sense of both financially supporting them and concealing their need from the public gaze.[5] The expression *covered families* became a euphemism for households who did not have the financial means to sustain themselves.

Against this background, this chapter turns to men selling small commodities, such as sweets and gum; textile workers who are struggling to get by; and women with families to provide an overview of the different ways in which people who are out of money conceal or tactically expose their need. Downplaying need and rejecting support sometimes serves as a sign of shyness and piety. At other times, it is an expression of irony (hinting at deeper layers of despair). Referring to Islam and keeping up an ironic sense of humor allow people to hold on to their dignity in social interactions. For those at the social margins, however, the everyday struggle to balance dignity with fighting for economic survival can be very tough.

The Tactics of Concealing Need

People without means use different tactics to conceal their needs. Families, for instance, offer aid to conceal signs of neediness among their relatives. The latter, however, sometimes reject such gifts to pretend they do not need support. For Layth, a machine operator working in one of Nablus's many sewing workshops producing clothes for Israeli merchants, looking after relatives was a central part of life. He often took care of his grandfather—changing his clothes and helping him into bed—and when one of his paternal relatives was in the hospital, he looked after him for months. Layth described the situation of another relative: "My paternal aunt is married to a poor husband. He sells vegetables from a moving cart that he pushes through the alleys, but he makes very little money from this. Sometimes people in the neighborhood pay much more than the official price when buying products from him. They know that he is poor through asking around about him in the neighborhood." Realizing that his aunt was struggling to get by, he sometimes helped her out during the time of year when Muslims remind one another to give zakat and be lenient in their financial dealings with others: "During Ramadan, I bring her money or food. Her brothers and their sons also give to her. As I am her brother's son, I do so as well. Usually, my aunt first rejects what we offer. She does not make it easy to give something to her, but then, we normally force her to keep it, and she accepts."

People in need tend to explain such rejections with their own shyness. The vast majority of people in need that I talked to insisted that they feel shy (*bistaḥū*, literally "make themselves shy") to openly accept support or to ask anyone for support. Some of them explicitly framed this as a matter of Muslim piety—or a pious display of shyness (*ḥayā'*). Others practiced modesty simply by concealing their own material need from the gaze of others to hold on to their own honor and dignity. Through the embodiment of shyness, those in need sought to shift the responsibility to cover need onto their relatives and neighbors.

Refraining from asking for or refusing to accept support—as Layth's aunt was trying to do—marks a kind of autonomy and piety. This echoes the role modesty plays in Abu-Lughod's ([1986] 2016) analysis of the "honor code" among Bedouins in the Sinai. She discusses how those in a position of weakness deal with the shyness they feel in the presence of more powerful people on whom they are dependent. Against this background, she argues that people reclaim a sense of autonomy and honor by defining their own shyness as modesty. For speaking about modesty, the Bedouins use the Arabic word *ḥasham*, which Abu-Lughod defines as "a form of self-control" in social interactions, aimed at preempting "the need for a show of strength by the powerful—a show that would reveal the subordinate's weakness. Initiated by the dependent, *ḥasham* is a voluntary act, a sign of independence . . . applying to the dignified way of being weak and dependent in a society that values strength and autonomy" (117). According to Abu-Lughod, *ḥasham* fuses deference with virtue and needs to be understood as the "honor of the weak" (117).

The issue of shyness has also emerged among Cairene women discussing Islamic texts in mosques as a means of living pious lives (Mahmood 2005). These women explicitly framed displays of shyness in terms of Muslim piety. As in Abu-Lughod's work, there is an open tension between virtue and deference. Mahmood found that her interlocutors actively enact gestures of shyness in their interactions in public. Repeated gestures of deference, such as lowering their gaze in the presence of men, allow them to inscribe habits in their bodies that are associated with the Muslim virtue of modesty, for which they use the word *ḥayā'* rather than *ḥasham*. Mahmood (2001, 212–217) interprets this cultivation of shyness as ethical self-fashioning and, therefore, a modality of agency.[6]

In Nablus, people in need sometimes display shyness to signal piety. Consider the interactions between a successful merchant and a recipient woman during a zakat transfer. One day, I accompanied Abu Farid, an affluent man working in real estate, on one of his regular visits to the household of a "covered family." Dressed in a suit, Abu Farid knocked on a metal gate in a side alley of the old city. Umm Maher, the wife of an unemployed man, opened the door and greeted him warmly. They exchanged invocations of God's blessings as Abu Farid and I stepped into the tiny and rundown apartment where the middle-aged woman lived with her husband and seven children. After we sat down, one of the children served coffee. Umm Maher told Abu Farid that her husband, who had been out of work for months, was currently out of the house. After a moment of silence, she added, "My husband is of the kind who is too shy [*bistaḥī*] to ask anyone for support." Tears appeared in her eyes. Abu Farid asked her why she had not called him earlier.

> **Umm Maher:** "I was too shy [*istaḥayt*]!"
> **Abu Farid:** "You can always call me. I will always provide you with food."
> **Umm Maher:** "You are a dear brother to me, Abu Farid. May God preserve you!"

During the conversation, Umm Maher quickly moved from shedding tears to praising God, smiling, and kindly laughing. Before leaving, Abu Farid gave her money to buy food for a few days and reminded her to get in touch with him if she was facing another difficult situation. She smiled and invoked God's blessing and protection for him. When we got back to his black Mercedes, Abu Farid called a shopkeeper and asked him to deliver a parcel filled with rice, vegetable oil, sugar, coffee, tea, eggs, flour, canned tomatoes, white cheese, and dried thyme to her.

By drawing the attention to her husband's refusal to ask for support, Umm Maher displayed the Islamic virtue of modesty (*ḥayā'*), highlighting both his piety and self-respect.[7] By presenting herself and her husband as shy, Umm Maher "gives an account of herself" and establishes her ethical "worth in the eyes" and "ears" (Keane 2015, 138) of her interlocutor. One could adopt a cynical reading and reduce the display of such pious self-restraint to a tactic of those in a position of weakness. Or one could interpret this as a part of the ethical self-fashioning of people struck by poverty. I suggest that it is both, a way of convincing visitors that they are "the right kind of poor" to receive zakat or sadaqa while also holding on to a certain self-worth in interactions with people who are more affluent than they are.

References to Islamic discursive categories when giving and receiving allows those in need to reframe their shyness as a sign of Muslim piety. Presenting oneself as modest is, therefore, a way of managing the impression (Goffman 1959) one makes on (potential) givers of zakat. Concealing one's own material want can turn into a display of piety through the embodiment of shyness, patience, self-restraint, and modesty. Families sometimes go without food for several weeks—staying at home and being dizzy. In the living room of a poor household in the old city, where guests—as well as potential zakat givers—are received, I came across a tableau on the wall with the following text written with golden beads: "I am going to be patient [sa'aṣbur] until the patience [ṣabr] falls short [ya'ajiz 'an] of my patience. And I am going to be patient until God hears [ya' dhana] my request [amrī]. And I am going to be patient until patience knows that I am enduring something [ṣābir 'ala shay'in] firmer [amarra] than patience."

This poster seems to provide visitors with an insight into the inner speech of the inhabitants and, therefore, a display of their cultivation of patience. In this sense, the text on the poster is both a sign for visitors and an act of self-care when recited by the inhabitants. The poster is a way of convincing visitors that the family living in this household is the "right kind of poor" (Mittermaier 2019, 108) to receive zakat or sadaqa while also holding on to a certain moral autonomy and dignity in interactions with people who are more affluent.

By not asking anyone for support, people without money display their trust in God. This impulse "not to ask" seems stronger among people threatened with slipping into poverty than among people who have been dependent on others for a long time. In a park, the mother of a family living in a refugee camp near Nablus explained to me how painful it was for her and other families to be sliding into poverty: "There is a lot of fear of falling into severe poverty and constant dependency on others. The worst aspect of this is the feeling of humiliation that goes along with it. I don't like asking rich people for aid. We [my family] are from the kind that is too shy to take aid. I feel shy [bastaḥī]." When

I asked her what she felt shy about, she answered, "The shyness of religion [*ḥayā' ad-dīn*]! We rely on God. God protects [or covers]."

The word *ḥayā'* is translated as "modesty" (Meneley 1996; Mahmood 2005, 23, 100–104, 155–161). It also means that one is able to show that one is shy and ashamed in a pious way. In English, *shame* has both an active (cultivated by the person) and a passive (inflicted onto a person by someone else) meaning. The Arabic term *ḥayā'* describes the active aspect of shame, the ability to feel and display shyness in given situations.[8] Appearance to others is key. The display of feeling ashamed in relations with others is central to one's constitution as a person. Drawing on research in a conservative Yemeni town in the 1990s, Meneley (1996, 81–96) argues that the active display of shyness appears in different contexts, such as piety, deference, sexuality, and family.[9] Shame does not merely consist of refraining from need (or desire).[10] It involves acknowledging desire, containing it, and perhaps transforming it.

Notwithstanding, destitute people need to present themselves in a positive light in front of potential givers. In Mittermaier's (2019) account of zakat practices in Cairo, doing so involves performing one's own suffering by exposing bodily signs of need or purposefully refraining from thanking the donor—for instance, by taking food from a Sufi soup kitchen and silently walking away. In Nablus, being the right kind of poor appeared to be more connected with embodying signs of shyness by refraining from asking and thereby displaying one's piety. This difference between Cairo and Nablus appears to relate to the much greater anonymity in the Egyptian metropole than in the old town of a small Palestinian city.

Exposing Need: The Tactics of Those without Money

Conversational references to honor and piety create a moral pressure to cover need. People often dispersed financial worries by saying that "God covers" (*allah yustur*), a statement also serving as a reminder to make sure that everyone is taken care of. The moral pressure becomes more explicit when people make their own need visible in front of others to shame them into giving. My interlocutors described this practice of laterally disciplining others to give as "making a scene" (*iḥrāj*). Umm Maher told me how she resorted to such tactics to get an affluent relative to provide their daughter with financial support:

> My husband's relatives do not help us save in situations where they fear being publicly embarrassed. One of our daughters attends university. She has always gotten very high grades. Some time ago, I managed to get some of my husband's relatives to ask Hajj X [a direct relative of her husband] to support

our daughter. The Hajj is an influential and wealthy man in the city. A group of our relatives went to him on our behalf and publicly pressured him. Given the risk of embarrassment, the Hajj promised to pay our daughter's student fees, but then he stopped after one semester and we had to get into debt with our neighbors. Now, our daughter has to walk to university every day and has no money to spend there. This scandalizes [*faḍaḥ*] her and her father!

In this context, making a scene consists of creating a social situation where the social standing of the more affluent party in an interaction is at risk and the duty to cover need becomes a matter of decency. This pressure to cover need remained implicit most of the time, however.

Irony among Textile Workers

Many sewing workshops in the West Bank produce clothes for Israeli entrepreneurs who import Chinese textiles. On traffic junctions in the West Bank that are accessible to both Palestinians and Israelis, they then hand these textiles over to a man from Nablus who owns a sewing workshop. Workshop owners mostly employ immediate and extended family members. They produce clothes according to the models provided by the Israeli partner.[11] The young men employed by a workshop that I often spend time with earned between fifty and seventy shekels per day (between ten and twelve dollars). Their employment was unsteady and depended on the volatile demands of the Israeli partner. When there was nothing to do, some of the sewing workers sold goods from wooden carts in the old city markets. Most of them were unmarried, and they often struggled to make enough money to get by. They decorated the walls of their workshop in an old garage with advertisements for American chocolate bars and stickers with Islamic messages. A piece of white paper showed a poem full of references to the Islamic texts:

> In the name of God, the most gracious, the dispenser of grace. Keep with the fear of God [or piety; *taqwā allah*] if you are oblivious, He generates for you the provisions from [a place] you do not know. And how [can you be] afraid of poverty when God is the Provider [*rāziq*]? He has already provided [*razaqa*] for the bird and the whale in the sea. . . . You [will] fade away from this world [*duniyā*] and when the night wraps itself around you, you do not know whether you will live until dawn. How many healthy [persons] died without a cause? How many sickly [persons] lived an animated life through an [entire] era? How many an adolescent reached the evening and woke up

smiling while his [funeral] shrouds in the unseen were moving [from one body to the next] and he did not know? And regarding he who has lived [until he reached] a thousand and two thousand [years], inevitably a day [will come] on which he will be moving to the tomb.

This poem seeks to dissipate the fear of poverty and reminds readers to have faith in God in spite of adverse situations. However, the young men in the workshop were, in different ways and to differing degrees, committed to practicing Islam. Some would pray and fast; others would skip these practices and instead ascribe more value to being decent and helpful in their interactions with others. In spite of this variance, the workers rarely criticized one another over such issues. Matters of piety and worship were largely left to the individual, as interfering in such matters could be considered an intrusion (*tadakhul*) and an attack on the other's sense of autonomy.

Young male textile workers often exposed their financial need metaphorically or by subtly conveying despair. In their everyday interactions, they used Islamic expressions less extensively than older folk. Describing their own situation, they often resorted to irony. When asked how they were doing—"[What is] your situation [*waḍ'a-k*]?"—they answered in various ways. The classic reply was "The praise be to God [*al-ḥamdu li-llah*]," communicating that life might be difficult but that one is holding on. However, they often used other expressions, such as "We are rolling on [*dāḥilīn*]." By this, they meant rolling like the wheels of a car that has run out of gasoline, as one of them explained: "The car continues rolling even if there is nothing inside it that can move it." I also heard the following expressions referring to the fact that one is out of money: *ṭafrān* ("broke"; literally "in the air"); *mamsūḥ* ("blank"; meaning "penniless"); and *dāyikh* ("dizzy," because of not being able to eat). Other expressions provided information of a more relational nature. The expression "under pressure" (*maḍghūt*) was often employed. It means that one is short of money and under pressure from different sides because one cannot meet some of one's obligations. When these pressures increased, the men would say that they were being "choked" (*makhnūq*).[12] Finally, to indicate financial distress, they used expressions that described people's appearance. "Sooty" (*musakham*) characterizes someone who does not have enough money to take care of his or her looks. This can happen to young workers who go without work for a long time and do not receive support from any of their relatives. This terminology indicates the importance of the flow of money through society and the consequences facing those who lack money. Perhaps the most dramatic term used is "fed up" (*zahqān*), meaning weary of running after money and work. While these expressions expose that one is in a tough situation, they do not suggest neediness but rather convey a sense of everyday struggle.

The following account describes the situational context behind a young man's self-designation as "fed up." Asking someone to pay back a debt is an exposure of need that can make the one who asks feel ashamed. It was early December, and the weather had become very cold in Nablus. Occasionally, it was snowing. Qusay, a sewing worker, had been in a bad mood for several days. He kept telling me that he was fed up. I called him up, and we met on a late afternoon. He was out of money. He told me that his plan for the evening was to get back a hundred shekels (roughly twenty to twenty-five dollars) he had lent to someone a month before. His maternal uncle had apparently talked Qusay into this. To find the debtor, Qusay wanted to visit his uncle and suggested that I come along. The uncle worked as a night watchman in a factory building. It was already dark when we got there. The factory was deserted. Qusay's uncle was sitting in front of a television next to the entrance, smoking cigarettes. We sat down next to him as he started calling the debtor. After half an hour, the debtor picked up. A few minutes later, a man with a mustache arrived. He wandered up and down the room. Qusay expected his uncle to put pressure on the man to make him pay back the debt, but this did not happen. The man with the mustache brought forward all kinds of excuses, including explanations that he had the money but that it was not in the city. After about ten minutes, the man with the mustache suggested that he go sell a few mobile phones so he could pay back his debt. He left and promised to be back soon. Qusay was frustrated. He took me on a small walk, where he told me that he would never ask and insist on getting the money if he were not totally broke and needing to work the next day. For this, he needed food and money for a taxi, as it might be snowing or raining. We went to a crowded food store in the eastern part of the city, where I bought dried yogurt, bread, and pickled eggplants stuffed with chili and nuts. We took the food back to Qusay's uncle and ate it with him. After dinner, the debtor showed up with another man. After greeting us, they started talking to Qusay's uncle in another corner of the room. Qusay whispered to me, "I am sure that the man brought somebody else along in order to make me feel too ashamed and shy [*'ashān astaḥī wa akhjal*] to continue asking him for the money. My uncle is supposed to ask him for the money, but he does not move!" Then the uncle, in the presence of everyone, confronted the man with the mustache and asked him to pay. The debtor then held a key in the air, saying that he had money far away somewhere in a house and that those were the keys to the house: "If you want, you can take these keys and go there to get the money." Qusay's uncle changed the subject and got back to small talk. Qusay was angry. He and I left without saying goodbye to the two men, who were still sitting in the back of the entry hall talking with his uncle. Before going home, I gave Qusay a bit of money to carry him through the next day.

Exerting pressure on wealthy persons by roping them into interactions that might embarrass them in front of others (*iḥrāj*) is a tactic that poor people can employ if they are bold enough, but it cuts both ways. Asking someone to pay back a debt is in itself an open display of need, which can make the creditor feel ashamed in the presence of others. In the scene above, Qusay was obliged to reveal his own neediness. The other man brought a third party to the meeting to make Qusay shy away from insisting further. The tactics of his creditor succeeded. Maintaining his honor and dignity in this situation was so important for Qusay that he refrained from taking further steps to extract the amount owed to him.

The Everyday Struggle for Dignity

Instead of openly asking for help, begging, or shaming others into providing for their needs, many people without a job or other form of livelihood attempt to sell extremely cheap commodities on the streets or in marketplaces. This practice reveals need but does so in a way that the counterparts in the interaction can pretend to be buying something rather than making a gift to a person in need. Sales of cheap commodities usually take place in precarious spaces in the market that the surrounding business owners concede to people in need. Such arrangements are often temporary and can be lost at any time because the police sometimes prevent such activities. People in need claim their right to sell these commodities by insisting on their "rightful share" according to the Quran. Through the sale of sweets, wild sage, or religious stickers, some people can reconnect to the flow of wealth through the markets and access a share of God's material provisions. Consider the following accounts of how those at the social margins invoke Islamic texts to defend their selling spaces when facing the police.

Stickers with Islamic Texts

The practice of selling stickers with Islamic texts was widespread. They appeared almost everywhere. People put them on doors, cars, factory machines, or carts in the market to protect themselves from misfortune. One midafternoon on a hot day in July during Ramadan, I saw two teenagers on a sidewalk selling small stickers with verses from the Quran. I felt dizzy from the fasting and the lack of water. Walking up to one of the young men, I signaled that

I would like to buy one of the stickers. He gave me one. I asked him, "What do I give you for this?" He replied, "Whatever erupts from yourself [*shū illī muṭalliʿ min nafs-ak*]! God will give to you [*allah byaʿaṭī-k*]." After I gave him three shekels for the sticker, he said, "May God support you [*allah ysʿada-k*]!"

By using the expression "erupts from yourself," the young man seemed to depersonalize our exchange. He implied that this transaction was also a matter between God and me. God would recompense me for the amount I would pay to purchase the sticker. This allowed the young man to widen the framing so that covering his financial need was no longer the central purpose of our transaction.

Transactions where such cheap commodities change hands rest on a delicate balance of mutual respect that protects the public appearance of everybody involved. A wrong word or gesture can disrupt this balance and lead to intense reactions capable of disgracing either side of the deal, as in the scene with the old man in the café at the beginning of this chapter.[13]

Gum at a Traffic Light

People sometimes cite Islamic texts to mitigate the shamefulness associated with need. Sales are often accompanied by expressions such as "May God open [this world] in front of your face." The person passing by can either accept and engage in the transaction or refuse and pronounce one of the following expressions: "God make it easy for you [*allah yassir l-ak*]"; "God protects [in the sense of covering need; *allah yustur*]"; or "May [you] be in God's eye [*bi ʿayn allah*]."

I observed such an exchange one day in January, when a friend was giving me a lift. We stopped at a traffic light. Two young boys between six and ten years old came running from a street corner to offer chewing gum to the people sitting in the cars. The car windows were open. My friend, who was driving, politely said to one of the boys that he did not want any gum. The boy smiled at him and said, "May God open [this world] in your face [*allah yiftaḥ-hā fī wujh-ak*]!" The traffic light turned green, and we drove off.

Later, a wealthy man looking after several poor families in Nablus introduced me to the mother of these boys. She was a widow without any means of support. By selling gum or Islamic stickers at the traffic light not far from her house, her boys contributed to the family's finances. When the light turned green, the boys would usually hide between the cement columns of a nearby construction site so that the police would not catch them. The mother told me, "Selling gum or Islamic stickers to cars at the traffic light is illegal, sure. However, from what should we live? This makes a few shekels every day. Down the street, some boys have been stealing shoes from the entry of a mosque. Praise be to God that my boys are not doing this! The problem is that people in the cars complain to the police. The police come and take my boys to the station. They intimidate and beat them, so they would not go continue to sell stuff at the traffic light." Invoking God, the mother claimed a moral right for her boys to carve out a space in the public sphere and sell extremely cheap commodities to help sustain their household.

Reciting the Quran to Claim a Selling Space

Suleiman, a man from another West Bank town, came to Nablus almost every day to sell wild sage harvested from the arid hills. As an outsider to Nablus, he struggled to find a place in the markets of central Nablus where he could sell his dried sage twigs. For a certain time, a wealthy and influential man procured a space for him, but the arrangement did not last. Suleiman was a fast talker and continuously wove verses of the Quran and sayings attributed to Prophet Mohammed into his speech. One day, he told me that he had had problems with the police. They tried to remove him from his selling spot, saying that it was part of the sidewalk and that he had no right to use it for commercial purposes. He claimed to have eventually obtained the protection of the mayor and explained that he had made himself a reputation by reciting the Quran with a loud and beautiful voice in public. Apparently, an imam from a nearby mosque confirmed that his ability to recite the Quran was extraordinary.

I often saw Suleiman when passing at this street corner. After sunset, he would usually move his bags with sage twigs next to a famous sweets and coffee place in central Nablus where people tolerated him as well. I had another conversation with him later on. He was sitting on the same stone step wearing jeans and a black leather jacket. His woolen sweater had several holes. When I asked him how he was doing, he said, "Pray on the Prophet and the anxiety dwindles away." I asked him where that verse was from. "This is from me," he replied. Suleiman went beyond merely citing the Quran; he wrote and recited his own pious poetry.

Movement in the office behind our backs interrupted our conversation. A very old man came out the office door. Suleiman helped him get into a car. Then he explained that this was the owner of the entire commercial building:

> He bought the land a long time ago and is now very rich. He uses the office behind us as a space from where to administer all his possessions in Nablus. One day, I was reciting the Quran in the streets when this man walked up to me and wanted to give me some money. I refused to take it and asked him instead for a tiny bit of space to sell sage. This wealthy man started letting me

use this little stone step in front of his office as a selling spot. By now, I have a good relationship with everybody around here. Even police and Palestinian security services are buying sage from me. They have all gotten used to me.

This statement shows how Suleiman's initial rejection of support and his ability to recite the Quran provided him with a spot to present his wild sage to potential customers. A few weeks later, Suleiman disappeared from the street corner. Months later, I ran into him in the eastern market of Nablus, selling sage from a much less lucrative spot, squeezed between two large vegetable stores. When I asked how things were going, he said that he had had many problems but refused to tell me what had happened. Suleiman's account illustrates the struggle and eventual failure to hold on to a selling spot by displaying signs of piety and reciting the Quran. Possibly, the self-made style of his pious poems raised suspicions.

The Entry of the Mosque as a Protected Selling Spot

Finally, people selling cheap commodities from carts can use the entryways of mosques during prayer time as a stable spot to sell their goods. In front of the Jamal Abdel Nasser Mosque in central Ramallah (another West Bank city), there was a big square where people held huge quantities of vegetables for sale next to secondhand kitchen supplies recovered from Israel. Stone stairs led up to the gate of the mosque. At the bottom of the stairs, a young man with a little cart was selling ʿarīsa, sweets made from semolina and sugar. He invited me to sit down on the stairs. As prayer time was approaching, people were already slowly dropping into the mosque. We relaxed and chatted. Throughout our conversation, several boys working in the market as carriers came over to buy sweets from the young man, one portion for a shekel. The semolina was spread out on a large metal plate covered by black plastic to protect it from flies, dust, and the sun. The man cut it into parallelograms with a scraper and handed a few pieces to the boys. The young man had a degree in medical laboratory work. As he could not find a job in that sector, he had fallen into poverty. I asked him whether he paid taxes for selling goods from his cart. He said:

> No. The overseers from the municipality know me and let me be, as long as I remain on the move with my cart. I cannot put the cart anywhere stable, except for at the entry of the mosque during prayer times. When the prayer ends and people pour out of the mosque, I sell to them. The police would not interfere when people come out of the mosque after prayer. When the people have left, I stay on for a bit, but I have friends everywhere around here. They warn me as soon as the market overseers from the municipality show up.

In this case, the entry of the mosque provided a somewhat stable selling spot during prayer times because the police feared that people would find it indecent if they harassed a young man struggling to get by while others were praying next to the scene.

Discussion: Shyness, Piety, and the Limits of Dignity

This chapter has laid out the various ways in which people without means navigate the pressures arising from their financial situation in social interactions with more affluent people. Material want often remains implicit, a matter of subtle signs that require tactful responses from those who detect them. My findings echo Perdigon's (2015) observations about the reticence of impoverished Palestinians in refugee camps in Lebanon to speak about their own situation in terms of poverty. His interlocutors chose indirect ways of disclosing their own situation, by describing problems, such as damp walls, failing arteries, or demotivated children, as something political (*shī siyāsī*) or by recounting their own gestures of refusing to accept support offered to them. Rather than explicitly addressing their own need, people without means in Nablus also prefer to speak about their own efforts to refrain from asking for help.

Building on ethnography from Egypt and Yemen discussing modesty and shyness, I suggest that embodying such virtues (as a display of Muslim piety) allows people to hold on to dignity and a sense of moral equality before God in spite of the financial inequality in their community.[14] We should neither underestimate nor overestimate the role of piety and virtues such as modesty, self-restraint, and shyness. However, the struggle for dignity is often fraught with difficulty. The tension between irony in the talk of young men and the despair that such ironic statements sometimes conceal adds a different twist to the dynamics of everyday interactions involving people who are financially broke. Moreover, people in need can also be tricksters playing a game to gain benefits.[15] During my fieldwork, I met a man selling religious texts on a street corner making quite a bit of money from it. Locals said that this was all show for people from other towns visiting Nablus to shop. They believed the man did not really care about either honor or piety.

While references to Islamic texts and the space of the mosque allow people in need to claim selling spots and tap into the movement of wealth through the markets, these arrangements are often temporary and precarious. Selling cheap commodities to survive while maintaining one's dignity is tough and has limits. The Tunisian Revolution of 2010–2011 allegedly started with the self-immolation of Mohamed Bouazizi, a young man selling vegetables from a mobile cart in a Tunisian small town to provide income for his widowed mother and his siblings. His suicide was an expression of despair after the police repeatedly tried to close his business. Bouazizi became a symbol of the revolution, and the call for dignity was one of its central demands.

In Nablus, the social duty to cover the needs of people in one's surroundings arises from a general concern for decency in everyday interactions. People sometimes expose their need in semipublic settings to discipline relatives into supporting them. This social duty to cover need aligns with the Islamic obligation to give zakat. The next chapter turns to how givers deal with the sensitivity of need when confronting receivers of zakat in face-to-face interactions. Explicit practices of giving zakat and sadaqa in Nablus require great tact and discretion as they aim at providing a certain degree of financial stability to poor households through more or less steady streams of wealth.

4

The Piety of Giving

Modeling Direct Zakat Interactions

Affluent people have a social duty to cover the needs of people in their proximity. While the obligation to give often arises from relations, givers frame their giving as piety and declare their gifts to be zakat or sadaqa. Not taking care of one's relatives or neighbors in need can seriously damage a person's or a family's reputation. Layth often worried that his relatives might show signs of material want to the public gaze. When his cousin Ahmed was depressed and out of work, he brought him to a Sufi sheikh running an old city mosque. The sheikh tried to heal the young man, without success. Ahmed continued to spend his days at old city mosques, where he slept in shady corners. Whenever Layth saw him sitting around like this and staring into the air, he was annoyed. The situation deteriorated, as Layth recalled: "Ahmed started neglecting his appearance. We [Layth and his relatives] were all exposed [*infaḍaḥ-nā*]. My uncles and I gave Ahmed new clothes and money, but he would not change anything. I started threatening him, in order to force him to take care of himself. We started fighting. At the end, the sheikh [the same who did the healing] in our neighborhood needed to intervene and reconcile us." Layth's reactions to his cousin illustrate how intense measures to prevent the visibility of need can be.

The obligation to cover the need of people in one's proximity is not only a matter of caring for the autonomous and honorable appearance of families and neighborhoods but also a matter of being a good Muslim. My interlocutors cited a saying attributed to the Prophet emphasizing that one should start giving first to everyone in one's proximity: "The relatives [or those who are near] are first in [what is generally] recognized [as good practice] [*al-aqrabūna awlā bi-l-ma'rūf*]." The most proximal people are one's own family members.

People who fail to take on the responsibility of covering the needs of their family can become socially despised (*ḥaqīr*). A man in such a situation who spent the little money he had on smoking water pipes rather than on his family told me that he fears his own relatives and suffers from his loss of social respectability, especially in such a small city, where no one can remain anonymous. In this sense, the Islamic obligation to give as a condition for being a virtuous Muslim—rooted in the concepts of zakat and sadaqa—aligns with a certain social compulsion (Dresch 1998, 116) to look after one's relatives.

The next most proximal families to be covered are one's neighbors. Several of my neighbors regularly brought me food, stating that looking after me and their other neighbors was a religious obligation. My interlocutors thought that sleeping in proximity to a person who goes to bed hungry deducts good deeds from one's "divine account" and might jeopardize one's transition to paradise. At the same time, they assumed that covering the needs of others would have a beneficial effect on their own lives. Layth's grandmother told me that God prolongs the life of those who are affectionate (*ḥanūn*) and help others in their proximity. This supports the idea that zakat is at once an obligation to God and a social duty to others.

The scope of direct or informal giving in Nablus is difficult to measure because of the discretion surrounding the issue. Many people said that, while zakat was vital to the survival of many poor households, researching such acts of giving was close to impossible because anyone receiving support would feel ashamed to talk about it. As already discussed in the previous chapter, a gift of zakat inevitably marks the recipient as needy, and it can have a wounding effect (Mauss [1925] 2016, 177).[1] Given the general reticence to talk openly about material need, the first problem that arises for zakat givers is how to locate and assess the needs of poor households in their proximity. The same reticence also made it difficult for me to study acts aimed at covering people's urgent needs. To avoid roping my interlocutors into shameful situations, I let myself be guided by the same ethics that my interlocutors relied on when looking out for poor households and assessing their needs. I gradually learned that my interlocutors were reading signs of need in the behavior of others to detect poor households and assess their degree of need. This sign reading relied on observations made during face-to-face interactions and visits. Signs were given implicitly and registered silently, to be passed on with great discretion to those wishing to give their zakat to a household in need. The point of discretion is to avoid embarrassing and shaming anyone by publicly exposing material want.[2]

While the previous chapter examined recipients' manifestations of piety, this chapter turns to how givers detect the needs of people who seek to conceal them and explores their gestures aimed at preserving the dignity of recipients. Direct zakat giving therefore involves an ethical work of presenting oneself to others in face-to-face interactions. Such self-presentation involves the strategic management of impressions (Goffman 1959) as an "ethical work on the self" (Keane 2015, 147) that in the case of zakat interactions links up with moral pressures exercised through lateral disciplining. I then explore how the direct giving of zakat and sadaqa aligns with the two models of zakat laid out in the introduction to this book. Givers see the zakat they give as divine money, as a share of the wealth provided by God that they are obliged to pass to people in need. At the same time, the giving of zakat also involves calculating what one owes to God and reflecting on the registration of acts of giving in God's accounting books, which keep track of people's good and bad deeds.

Detecting People's Needs

Reading the subtle signs of poverty in public is crucial for determining whether other people are eligible to receive zakat or sadaqa. Those wishing to give zakat usually look to women's gatherings, shopkeepers, or mosques to generate knowledge on material needs in Nablus. This knowledge is then discreetly shared among various social networks.[3]

The women my research assistant Marah interviewed told her that they would detect signs of need when visiting one another's homes by inspecting the state of the furnishings and occasionally going into kitchens to examine the contents of refrigerators. An empty refrigerator, for instance, was a clear sign of financial scarcity and incited giving. Maryam, a married woman living with her family in a village outside Nablus, one day went to visit one of her in-laws, a widow with three children. After some time, Maryam sneaked into the kitchen and saw that there was no food in the refrigerator. The next day, Maryam bought groceries and went to the widow's house to fill her refrigerator. The woman reacted with surprise: "Were you spying [*tfayyidī*] in my fridge?" Maryam replied, "No, I just wanted to get something out of the fridge when I visited you yesterday. Then I saw that it was empty." After this incident, Maryam called one of her wealthier relatives abroad and convinced her to start providing monthly payments for this widow and her three kids.

Other women could detect signs of need in public. Women living in villages would occasionally go to the central markets in Nablus and look around for women who appeared to be in need. One woman claimed to be able to spot financial distress by examining facial traits or bodily movements of strange women in the streets and looking for signs of worry or fatigue. When these women found a likely candidate for assistance, they would start talking to her. If it turned out that she was poor, they would try to help as much as they could afford. They claimed only to talk to other women in the street, never men. Occasionally, however, they would ask men shopkeepers in the old city if they knew of any poor women nearby who needed help. If there was one, they might go to her home and offer zakat or sadaqa.

Dina, a member of the Palestinian Parliament for the Fatah Movement, ran a charitable society in Nablus. She recognized that asking people directly whether they needed assistance often led nowhere, as many destitute families would tell their neighbors, "We do not need anything!" She recommended that potential zakat givers ask the "most influential lady of the neighborhood" (*sitt al-ḥāra*) if they wanted to know the whereabouts of poor households. According to Dina, these ladies play a leader role in the neighborhood. Other women show them reverence (*hayba*) and listen to them in important matters. An influential lady's position allows her to centralize information considered very sensitive. Everyone knows her, and everyone talks to her. Dina thought that such women are even "better than the Ministry of Social Affairs" as sources of information about the people in need, as they are aware of the tiniest details related to private matters.

Knowledge of poor households circulated swiftly among social networks in Nablus, even though most people were hesitant to reveal their needs. Outsiders like myself walking through the old city of Nablus would not think that many families behind the walls of these buildings had no access to regular meals or necessary medical services. A young man told me that very few people in Nablus knew the extent of poverty and the whereabouts of the poor families in the old city: "There are some respectable men of a certain age who know where they are. They are able to distribute zakat. Unmarried and young men like you and me cannot know such things." The men I talked to relied on interactions outside of homes to generate knowledge about households that had run out of money. The two main places for detecting signs of need were grocery stores and mosques. Nablus only had two large supermarkets, but street-corner shops selling groceries were widespread. These small grocery stores played an important role in the social perception of a family's material scarcity since shopkeepers were well situated to observe and interpret the consumption patterns of their customers. One day, for example, I was chatting with Kamal, the owner of a little grocery store who had spent many years working in the Arab Gulf. A small boy walked into the shop and asked him, "How many eggs can I get for two shekels?" Kamal silently placed three eggs in a plastic bag and handed them to the boy while taking two coins in return. After the boy left, Kamal turned to me and said, "Did you see this? This boy's family is broke. If they still had money, they would send him to buy a whole box of eggs to get a better price." Like many other shopkeepers, Kamal would keep track of the consumption patterns of his neighbors and, thereby, generate reliable knowledge about poverty in the vicinity. People's patterns of buying food allowed shopkeepers to infer the financial situation of families. While this information remained hidden to strangers moving through public space, shopkeepers administered this knowledge carefully, disclosing it tactfully to discreet givers. People wishing to give zakat often turned to shopkeepers such as Kamal to find families in need of support.

The mosque is another social sensor for financial hardship because it is a space where men struck by poverty can spend time when they do not have much else to do. In the mosque, one can pray, rest, and occasionally receive support from fellow Muslims. This meeting space allows merchants to socialize with men from poor households living in the old city. Merchants sometimes help these families by giving them money and helping them pay for medical operations.

The Ethical Work of Self-Presentation in Zakat Transactions

The extensive knowledge about poor households that was available among men's and women's social networks stands somewhat in contrast to statements insisting on the importance of discretion in zakat practice. For example, some of the women Marah interviewed claimed that they succeeded in keeping their own zakat transfers hidden from *anyone*, to protect the identity of the recipients from gossip in the neighborhood. Giving, however, can never remain entirely hidden.[4] A guidebook published in Nablus in 2001 (Nablus Zakat Committee 2001, 124–126) addresses various aspects of giving zakat. While recommending that one give in silence and hide the transaction, the text also states that there is no "embarrassment in showing [to others that one adheres to] the obligation of zakat under the condition that it does not [invoke] excessive flattery" and that giving zakat "is part of the [visible] signs [*dalā'il*] of faith and of the marks [*amārāt*] of piety" (125–126).

In direct zakat giving, givers embody piety and attend to the dignity of the receiver by concealing and depersonalizing transfers of wealth. This requires great tact on the side of the giver. Lack of tact invites scolding. Consider the following account of zakat giving in East Jerusalem (recorded and passed on to me by a friend) during Ramadan 2014. Before the celebration of the fast breaking at the end of Ramadan, Nawal and a group of young women living in the old city of Jerusalem began looking for needy families and collecting money to offer them some help. Through a friend, they heard about a poor family in Silwan, a predominantly Palestinian neighborhood on the outskirts of the old city of Jerusalem. The family lacked the funds to finish a renovation of their kitchen. As the money collected by the young women was not enough at first, they sent male friends to a craftsman to ask him whether he could renovate the kitchen for a lower price than usual. He refused. Then Nawal and her friends decided to dress up beautifully and pay a visit to the craftsman themselves. This time, the man immediately agreed to the suggested price and sent his workers, who quickly finished the renovation of the kitchen. In the end, one of the women who had joined the group shared a message on a social media site taking pride for having helped a poor family. Nawal was appalled and reprimanded her. According to Nawal, this woman started feeling ashamed every time they ran into each other somewhere. Nawal said that many people were boasting about their gifts to the poor these days, even though it was "forbidden in Islam" to do so. This illustrates how overtly taking pride in one's gifts is both impious and tactless.

For Abu Farid, mentioned in the previous chapter, giving zakat was part of a wider project of cultivating piety in his everyday life. He continually invoked God before stepping through a door or starting a car and claimed to spend hours in his office reciting the Quran—when he had no other work. Other men in the city sometimes made jokes about his taste for visiting people in need and looking after them, but for Abu Farid, these visits and encounters were part of the cultivation of Islamic piety.[5] Reflecting on his relationship to Umm Maher and her family, Abu Farid stated, "She sometimes calls and asks me for help. Her husband never asks. In fact, I asked him several times whether he needs anything, but he always says no. This is a father who sticks to his family and to his responsibility. There are many men who, in a situation like this, run away from their responsibilities. He is different. His manliness and his dignity forbid him to take aid from others. He has self-restraint ['*iffat al-nafs*]."

When I asked him about the behavior expected from families in need, such as that of Umm Maher, Abu Farid cited the Quran (2, 273): "[And give] unto [such of] the needy who, being wholly wrapped up in God's cause, are unable to go about the earth [in search of livelihood]. He who is unaware [of their condition] might think that they are wealthy, because they abstain [*aghniyā' min at-ta'affuf*] [from begging]; [but] thou canst recognize them by their special mark: they do not beg of men with importunity. And whatever good you may spend [on them], verily, God knows it all."

By referring to the Quran when speaking about his interactions with families in need, Abu Farid exercised a certain disciplinary power suggesting that recipients *should* present themselves as modest by "abstaining from begging" and by concealing their need. This case illustrates that lateral disciplining can work in both directions. While those in need can occasionally shame the affluent side into giving, the givers of zakat also discipline poor households by expecting them to present themselves as worthy recipients. Abu Farid's cultivation of piety through zakat requires him to give to people displaying the qualities of the "right kind of poor" as defined in the Islamic tradition. Consider the work of Abu Hamid al-Ghazali, a Muslim Aristotelian intellectual living in late eleventh-century Baghdad—work that resonates with the ethnographic material presented in this chapter and the previous one. Ghazali ([1097] 1966, 47–55) holds that the giver of zakat needs to seek a worthy recipient according to a list of desired qualities, including piety or devotion to the affairs of the Hereafter, devotion to knowledge and learning, honesty and acceptance of God's unity, being "unknown, having concealed his need, and not much given to complaint and grumble," being a person "of magnanimity who has lost his wealth but still keeps his magnanimous qualities and maintains his poise and self-restraint," being a person who has to support a family or sick and disabled people, and, ideally, being a relative of or close kin to the giver.

Givers as well as receivers of zakat engage in the ethical work of presenting themselves. The disciplinary effect of displays of piety in zakat transactions, however, cuts both ways. While those without money are disciplined to present themselves as virtuous, the affluent risk tainting their own reputation if they fail to cover the needs around them. Moreover, if givers brag about their generosity and treat recipients without tact, they can lose their piety.

Exemptions from the Requirement to Display Piety

Certain kinds of people without means are exempt from the obligation to embody shyness and conceal their needs in public. My interlocutors call them the helpless (*masākīn*). These are people who are not in a mental or physical state to care for their own appearance. People locally known as such can walk into shops or restaurants and ask for tea or food without paying. At the same time, the presence of such people in the public sphere still invokes the obligation of family members to attend to their reputation. For example, the people running the Hammouz Café were kindhearted, open men who tolerated the presence of people in financial or mental distress inside the café. On a warm morning in June, a man of about sixty wearing a suit and a tie walked over to the table where I was sitting on the terrace of the Hammouz. He looked confused. The zipper of his trousers was open. He took a chair and sat down at my table, asking me whether he could sing something for me. It was about 8:00 a.m. As I hesitated to answer, the man started singing. Occasionally, he stopped to burst into laughter, attracting the attention of other people sitting on the terrace. Two waiters and the owner of the café came over to inquire what was going on. One of the waiters wanted to force the man to leave. The owner—a very kind man—disagreed and tried to enter into a conversation with the singing man. One of the waiters stated that the behavior and the looks of the singing man were shameful (*'ayb*), adding that this man's son was respectable (*muḥtaram*) and that his father's demeanor would scandalize him (*yfḍaḥ-hu*).

This added a new twist to the situation, bringing questions of honor and reputation into play. The three men quickly agreed on kindly asking the man to leave the café until he could calm down. They convinced him to get up and gently guided him to the exit. The man turned to me, saying, "Didn't *you* ask me to sing?" I did not know what to say. There seemed to be nothing that I could do to change the situation. The waiters had implied that an absent man's respectability (that of the singing man's son) was at stake—and this required that the singer be diligently guided to the exit of the café and asked to calm down outside. Half an hour later, he showed up again. He remained quiet and sat down in a corner of the café without attracting further attention. Tact and kindheartedness enabled the waiters to deal with signs of openly visible need—in this case, the scruffy appearance and uncontrolled behavior—of a man without tainting the reputation of his relatives. The waiters explicitly cared for the honor of the man's relatives by preventing the scene from attracting too much attention.

The Two Models of Zakat in Action

Face-to-face interactions between givers and receivers require both tact and an embodiment of piety. The two models of zakat as both (1) the passing on of God's wealth to those in need and (2) a transaction registered in a divine system of bookkeeping bringing forth a heavenly reward allow us to understand how tact and piety are connected in practice. Both models directly manifest themselves in the ethnography of zakat transfers in Nablus.

Zakat as Passing on God's Wealth

To avoid embarrassing recipients and exposing their needs, givers tend to obscure their own role as givers by highlighting that the real source of a gift of zakat (as well as all wealth) is God. This directly aligns with the model of zakat as passing on God's wealth. One day in 2014, my research assistant Marah Az joined a group of women friends and relatives for coffee and an afternoon chat in an apartment in Nablus. Khadija, one of the wealthier women in the group, described to Marah how she usually gives zakat or sadaqa during such gatherings. When the gathering took place at the home of women in financial difficulty, Khadija would discreetly slip a bunch of bank notes under a pillow on a chair in a corner of the apartment. Saying goodbye on the doorstep, Khadija would kiss the host's cheeks, whisper in her ear that she had left something for her, and point to the chair. Then she would say, "May God bless you." The host would reply, "And may God bless you!" Khadija would add, "May God preserve you and your children!" After the host reciprocated this wish as well, Khadija would leave. When Marah asked Khadija whether she gave zakat secretly so as to avoid making her hosts feel ashamed in the eyes of the others, Khadija replied, "There is nothing shameful [*'ayb*] about zakat. Zakat is the wealth of God [*māl allah*]. People should cooperate with one another. People need to live. The money given to the poor is from God. It is not really our money. It is our duty to distribute it." In this statement, Khadija downplays the fact that openly visible need is shameful—even if her actions suggested that it is, as Marah aptly observed. In her reply, Khadija presented herself as a mere channel of God's generosity. By effacing her own role in the circulation of God's material provisions, she displayed modesty and appeared to shape herself "into a medium for God's will" (Mittermaier 2019, 140). Zakat in this context was qualified as divine money, which allowed Khadija to mitigate the potential for her gift to bring shame to her friend.[6] In an attempt to acknowledge the fundamental equality of the recipient and herself before God, Khadija foregrounded the model of zakat according to which humans are mere channels of God's material provision.

Most of the women interviewed by Marah stated that giving with hidden gestures was common during visits. They discreetly slipped money into clothes and under pillows or placed it in the recipient's hand when saying goodbye. Rather than expecting gratitude, the women accompanied their gifts by invocations of divine blessings that were reciprocated by the receivers. These wishes constituted givers and receivers as recipients of God's sustenance. The utterings and gestures used in face-to-face interactions, therefore, enacted zakat as divine wealth, a materialization of divine blessing and an obvious sign of His generosity and ability to "cover" everyone's needs. Such invocations of God mark a certain "mutuality and equality" (Henig 2019, 228) in Islamic acts of giving that, in certain brief moments, are able to eclipse real differences of wealth and class. Some women givers and receivers were actually becoming close friends over the years. In such relations, the givers framed what was given as zakat or sadaqa as a simple "present" (*hadiyah*) and an expression of friendship—even if they personally considered it zakat or sadaqa.

Women can play an important role when men try to efface their roles as givers to avoid affecting the honor of a male receiver. Several people told me that men give their zakat and sadaqa to women who distribute it for them without disclosing the identity of the giver. Kamal, the shopkeeper detecting need in his neighborhood, told me a story about how his wife helped him anonymize a gift. One of his former school friends had financial problems and struggled to care for his family. On the occasion of Ramadan, Kamal sent him new clothes for his children. When the friend found out where the gift was coming from, he sent the clothes back to Kamal as he did not want anybody to think of him as needy. Kamal then bought another set of children's clothes and gave them to his spouse, instructing her to find a discreet way to deliver them to his friend's wife, making sure that his friend would have no way of knowing where they were coming from. Only then was the gift accepted.

The model of passing on God's wealth also aligns with the injunction to give zakat and sadaqa in one's proximity. It is in immediate relations that zakat emerges as duty to both God and others in need. The women interviewed by Marah said they would give in concentric circles. After their children and their husband, they would care first for their parents and then for their sisters and brothers. Thereby, they sought to strengthen (1) the ties between people related through female lines of descent, which they sometimes refer to as the "bond of the womb" (ṣilat al-raḥm); (2) the solidarity in the neighborhood ('arṣa); and then (3) the solidarity beyond the neighborhood. Several women insisted that zakat was the obligation (farḍ) of the giver and the "rightful share (ḥaqq)" of the receiver. The Quran (93, 10) recognizes that the duty to give arises from relational pressures: "The one who asks [for help] is not to be turned away." Maryam, a woman interviewed by Marah who lived in a village with olive groves near Nablus, stated that during the harvest season, women from refugee camps came asking for olives and olive oil. They knew that many families in the villages had their own olive groves, and they would ask for the "zakat on olives"—their rightful share of the harvest. Maryam claimed that she would always give olives in such situations.

Marah's interlocutors stated that they gave sadaqa to fend off misfortunes, such as illnesses or accidents, affecting themselves or their families. A gift of sadaqa can protect from the "evil eye" and prevent misfortunes from recurring. Zakat and sadaqa are said to mitigate the envy or the grudges of people in one's proximity that can bring about misfortune. In this sense, people seek to affect their social relations through pious giving. Throughout the year, the women interviewed by Marah would give sadaqa whenever something bad happened to one of their family members, such as when a child had a very high fever, and they referred to a saying attributed to Prophet Mohammed: "Heal the sick among you with sadaqa"—by giving *on behalf* of a sick person. Moreover, the women thought that you can give sadaqa to prevent sinful behavior from spreading—after a sin has occurred in your proximity. Sometimes, they gave sadaqa when they felt that their family was facing bad luck.

The duty to pass on some of the wealth that one receives is enshrined in the practice of *zakat al-fitr*, whose payment is incumbent on everybody, even people without any wealth and minors. Due at the time of the breaking of the fast at the end of Ramadan, *zakat al-fitr* corresponds to one bushel, or about 2.2 kilograms, of the local staple food, or the equivalent in cash (Benthall and Bellion-Jourdan 2009, 9). This was widely practiced in Nablus during the month of Ramadan. People made sure that everybody could be in the position of a giver at least once during Ramadan and experience themselves as a vessel of the flow of divine provisions.

The image of zakat as an act of passing on God's wealth captures acts of giving that emerge from social relations. The image of zakat as an act of trading with God, however, invokes the issue of calculating one's wealth and determining the rightful share one is obliged to give away as zakat and the divine accounting of good and bad deeds.

Zakat as a Loan to God in the System of Divine Bookkeeping

As a loan to God, a gift of zakat is registered as a good deed in a divine account from which the givers receive a reward in the Hereafter. As such, it is part of the ethical self-cultivation of givers. The idea of the loan brings calculative reason into play. If one fails to pay the correct amount, one does not live up to one's obligation to God and risks invalidating one's prayers. Zakat practice thus requires calculation. In Ramadan, the annual zakat payment is due. The mufti announces how much eighty-five grams of gold are worth in the locally used currencies that year and encourages Muslims to give away 2.5 percent of the wealth they own beyond this threshold as zakat.

The men and women Marah and I talked to calculated what they owed as zakat in different ways. Certain people used an online calculator similar to a tax declaration. Others listened to radio programs where Muslim scholars discussed how to calculate zakat on different agricultural products. Most of my male interlocutors stated that they did a rough calculation during Ramadan to get an idea of the amount they needed to extract from their possessions as zakat. Then they reflected on what they had been giving to others and started to be more generous with people in need. In the end, they tried to make sure to give more than the amount of zakat they owed and considered the rest to be sadaqa.

As wealth is often not owned by individuals, determining the correct amount of zakat owed by each member of a family can be challenging. Many of the women Marah interviewed calculated zakat on the wealth of their husbands and paid it on behalf of all the family members. Sometimes they also paid zakat on their bridewealth. Women who received regular allowances from children or relatives passed some of it on to others and considered this to be zakat, even if they did not have a lot of standing wealth. Certain bigger households put up boxes and had all the family members fill them with money during the entire year. At the end of Ramadan, they would open the box and give its contents to people in need. Dina told Marah that rich people would sometimes give her money to distribute among the poor. She recalled becoming active in zakat and sadaqa in elementary school, where she established a fund (*ṣandūq*) with the help of her family. She assembled her friends at school and managed to convince them to donate parts of their pocket money to this fund. After some time, Dina was able to buy sweaters and trousers and gave them to her teacher, who distributed them to the pupils in need.

The guidebook on zakat (Nablus Zakat Committee 2001, 126) recommends that the giver "heals himself through zakat" while "entrusting God with the calculation [*yaḥtasib*] of its reward" and "being conscious of the recompense [*ajr*] of this extraordinary [form of] worship." The women interviewed by Marah stated that they gave zakat to protect themselves from hellfire. One woman said, "When I give zakat my soul relaxes. Zakat . . . saves human beings in the Hereafter." Another woman cited a saying ascribed to the Prophet: "Protect yourself from the fire of hell even if it is only through offering a date." The extent that zakat evokes people's transition into the Hereafter—which they assumed to undertake as individuals—foregrounds the first model of zakat as a "loan to God." In this sense, accruing good deeds in the divine account is a "technology of the self" (Foucault 1997, 225; discussed in the introduction).[7] As a "loan to God," giving zakat is part of such a technology of the self. As good deeds, gifts of zakat "count" on Judgment Day and possibly affect people's transition into the Hereafter.[8] This explains why people see giving zakat as a protection from hellfire.

Similarly to the women, my male interlocutors viewed zakat as influencing the transition of an individual giver into the Hereafter. According to a junior sheikh working for the Palestinian Authority, the practice of zakat affects the individual "heart":

> Zakat is worship. It is not to be imposed by force. It is between me and my heart and me and my reason [*'aql*], not between me and my pocket nor

between me and the ruler [al-ḥākim]. At the office of the mufti [where he worked], it is our job to inspire people's hearts [qulūb] [in a way to make them] stick to the five pillars of worship.... Zakat is purity and accretion. When I give zakat, I feel it in my heart. Zakat increases your divine account [ajr]. This account determines where you will be ranked in heaven. There are several levels of varying proximity to God.

With regard to the Hereafter, giving zakat was said to have a soothing effect on the heart (qalb), as it relieves fears of Judgment Day. According to my interlocutors, giving zakat can inspire an inner state of serenity (ṭum'ānīna). One of my interlocutors told me that giving zakat purifies the body of the giver and absolves him or her from guilt (ghafar al-dhanb). In his view, giving zakat is similar to healing an illness as it purifies a person from negative feelings.

The model of zakat as a transaction with God in a system of divine bookkeeping opens up the possibility of giving on behalf of others and transferring the divine merit of the gift to them.[9] When discussing sadaqa, my male interlocutors tended to cite the following saying ascribed to Prophet Mohammed: "When a human being dies, his work [in the world] is interrupted except with a view to [these] three: flowing sadaqa, [a body of] knowledge which [people] benefit from, or a son that invokes divine care for him." Flowing sadaqa is generally understood to be a steady flow of wealth for the benefit of the community that is set up on behalf of a deceased person. A classic example is the "water of the path" (mā' al-sabīl), or fountains, which are dedicated to deceased family members—often by sons for their fathers.[10] Refreshing travelers who are passing by the fountain, the water of the path is a perpetual stream of giving that increases the number of good deeds registered on behalf of the dead person.

Numerous fountains in Nablus provide water "from the soul" of deceased women or married couples. An engineer working for the municipality of Nablus explained that such fountains used to be established on land that had access to natural fountains or subterranean water channels:

> The water of the path practice changed when the water started to be supplied by the infrastructure offered by the municipality. The municipality accepts donations from people who want to build a fountain. The donation is then used to build the infrastructure, either a fountain or a water cooler. Once this is built, the municipality provides free water and free electricity for coolers. There is, for instance, a woman who donated for the building of a fountain from the soul of her deceased husband next to a supermarket. Nowadays, there are hundreds of such installations in Nablus, mainly in the

gathering places of collective taxis, schools, mosques, and in front of shops where they are generally provided with water and electricity by the shop owners themselves.

Such steady flows of sadaqa can also take other forms, such as regularly sustaining families with food or clothes. This can involve an agreement between a donor and a bakery to offer bread to poor households. Certain wealthy bakeries had a reputation for regularly providing families with free bread—along with food and clothes on special occasions. Moreover, flowing sadaqa can take the shape of printed text. According to the librarian at the municipal library of Nablus, people frequently offer the books of a deceased person to the library. A similar practice consists in offering a printed version of the Quran to a mosque. On the inside of the cover, the donors write that this copy of the Quran is flowing sadaqa from the soul of the deceased person, whose name they mention.

Calculative reasoning in zakat giving complements the idea of passing on God's material provisions. The image of a divine bookkeeping behind zakat and sadaqa hints at an ideal of a society in balance where everyone receives and everyone gives their rightful share. While this rightful share remains difficult to determine and the arithmetic of divine bookkeeping eludes human comprehension, calculative reasoning suggests that it is worth pursuing this ideal nonetheless. When in doubt, one should entrust God with divine bookkeeping and simply give a bit more.

Discussion: Inequality, Informal Zakat, and Piety

When reflecting on the problem of poverty and the differences in wealth among Palestinians (as well as in the wider Middle East more generally), my interlocutors rarely used the word *inequality* (*'adam al-musāwā*). More often, I heard statements that extreme concentrations of wealth wherever they may occur constitute a terrifying risk for the owners. A fortune may be contaminated with gains prohibited in Islam or attract divine punishment because its owner fails to pass on the "rightful share" as zakat—with possibly far-reaching and decisive consequences on Judgment Day. In this perspective, wealth is only a political or ethical problem if and to the extent that its owners disentangle themselves from the social and divine obligation to pay their share to others in need. This is a danger that people without wealth do not face, as they struggle for both economic survival and basic dignity as persons. Consequently, many of my interlocutors envisioned a society more committed to the precepts of Islam as one where everyone would pay their rightful share.

While zakat in Nablus did provide many poor households with a certain financial stability, it was not enough to cover people's perceived financial and medical needs in the absence of formal welfare structures. The owner of a butcher shop told me that many people in Nablus stayed at home and died there because they could not get access to medical treatment on time.

The imam of the Jamal al-Bayk Mosque in the old city concurred: "The city is in a very difficult situation. In the mosque, we encourage people to use their hands and their reason [*'aql*] to manage their lives. We encourage them to look for work—if need be—even in Israel. This is not enough, however. Many people in the mosque ask us for help, but all we can do is refer them to the different Islamic and non-Islamic aid organizations. The services that institutions are offering in Nablus are by far not sufficient to cover the need, especially in the field of medical care."

A junior sheikh working for the mufti of Nablus admitted that "the work of imams and sheikhs in mosques is very stressful. Many people suffer from the feeling of being crushed and defeated. They are burdened by numerous worries. The task of the imams is to make these people feel at ease with what they have."[11]

In spite of its limits, the informal practice of giving zakat and sadaqa acknowledges a socially distributed responsibility to look after people and cover their basic needs. This sense of responsibility arises from a social consensus that material want should not appear to the public gaze and that people are obliged to cover need through discreet gestures of pious giving. In fact, the care for how persons and gifts appear to the public gaze is at the center of zakat practice. It is on this level that lateral disciplining operates. This disciplining can oblige people to present themselves in certain ways, depersonalize gifts by obscuring their source and casting them as God's money, and pressure people into covering openly visible need in their proximity. Lived zakat practice involves both the care for one's standing with God with a view to a divine account of good and bad deeds determining one's position in paradise *and* the careful enactment of gestures and statements in interactions with others. As such, zakat gives rise to an ethical practice combining the care of the self (Foucault 1986) and the management of impressions in social interactions (Keane 2015, 147; drawing on Goffman 1959). In encounters between givers and receivers, the Islamic tradition (T. Asad 1986) emerges as a "discourse in face-to-face interaction" (Hacking 2004). In a place such as Nablus, it is difficult to retreat into a fully private sphere where one could cultivate a pious self that is detached from one's social roles and responsibilities in city life. This urges us to think of zakat practice beyond bourgeois distinctions between the private and public and to examine how Muslim piety embodied through hidden acts of covering need exceeds the individual.

Piety plays a key role in creating a sense of moral equality between givers and receivers. Invoking God's power has the effect of "depersonalizing" (Laidlaw 2000, 623) gifts of zakat and limiting the extent to which the gift is seen as a symbol for existing hierarchies. While such hierarchies are sometimes made explicit through gifts (for such a reading of exchange among Pakistani women in Britain, see Werbner 1990), Marah's and my interlocutors actively tried to prevent hierarchal relations from becoming explicit when giving. Consider this example from Morocco illustrating how far a commitment to Muslim piety can go to protect the dignity of recipients and to prevent social hierarchies from manifesting themselves through zakat. Spadola (2011, 89) conveys the following story that he heard from Mohammed, a man known as an exemplar of a good Muslim in his neighborhood in the old city of Fes:

> A few weeks ago, I stopped over there to see a poor family. They invited me in to sit down for dinner, but apologized that they had no bread. They have no money—not even for bread. I said I would come back in a moment with bread and walked to this corner store. They were sold out. It was very late—no more bread for the day. I know another family over on that street. I knocked, and the son said, come in, come in. I said, "I cannot. But do you have bread?" Yes, the son said. "Give me, please, two loaves," I said. I took the bread to the poor family. If one person has, it can be shared with another who doesn't. Even half a loaf is better than no bread. Last Friday, a friend said to me, "Mohammed, you should not be begging from people."

Mohammed adds that he never helps poor households for "applause." To protect the dignity of people in need, he is prepared to bear the shame of exposing such need by asking others for bread. He added that what counts for him in the end is that he remains able to respect himself. Such stories where piety overrules concerns with one's own honor allow someone to gain the reputation of being a "real" example of a good Muslim.

Invocations of God as the sole source of material provisions during direct encounters between givers and receivers allow people to "decenter" the agency of humans in acts of giving (Mittermaier 2019, 108, 181) by casting zakat as divine wealth. Inserting the flow of wealth into a wider imagination of the cosmos—as manifest in the different models of zakat—provides an explicit grounding for the responsibility of the affluent to give away a "rightful share" to those in need. This vision of the distribution of wealth through direct zakat giving resonated with the lifeworlds of many people struggling to make a living and to cover the needs of their relatives and neighbors. Many of my interlocutors were convinced that if all Muslims paid the amount of zakat they owed, everyone could benefit from God's material blessings. To some, this opened up a horizon for living good lives and practicing self-respect, dignity, and steadfastness in a context of otherwise opaque wealth flows and military occupation—where people felt that they had almost no realistic possibility of challenging a political order that curtailed their economic development (Turner and Shweiki 2014). The next chapter turns to an exploration of how this vision of God as Ultimate Provider and Arbiter manifests itself not only in zakat transfers but also in everyday financial transactions in the markets of Nablus.

5

The Ethics of Giving and Market Transactions

In Nablus, God is invoked as a third party not only in zakat giving but also in transactions (*mu'āmalāt*) in the market. This chapter explores everyday life in the city's markets, where we encounter sensitivities that are similar to the ones surrounding gifts of zakat and sadaqa. Discussing people's concerns with shame, the visibility of need, God's role as Provider of wealth and Bookkeeper, all of which come out of the ethnography of market life presented in this chapter, I argue that market transactions in Nablus unfold in a specific social context in which tensions can arise from a wider morality of giving and exchange (on which, see also Elyachar 2005, 139).

As in the transactions surrounding zakat, material need can also become visible in market transactions and be deemed shameful (*'ayb*). The urge to avoid any public sign that could be interpreted as being in need leads market sellers to reject payments from people they know. Such refusals to accept payment can give rise to a nervous shifting back and forth of coins between customers and sellers. Neither party wants to be seen in the role of recipient. People in the market are extremely hesitant about publicly accepting gifts because bystanders could interpret doing so as a display of need compromising the honor and autonomy of oneself and possibly also one's relatives. This suggests that gifts can be poisonous (Mauss [1925] 2016), in the sense of having a detrimental effect on the recipient. In ethnography from Middle Eastern contexts, the "poison" in the gift is often "relational" (Dresch 1998, 112), with implications of shame, autonomy, and honor.[1] The intensity and spontaneity with which market transactions turn into a contested act of giving in Nablus suggest the existence of a social "compulsion" to give (Dresch 1998, 116–117), similar to the relational pressures that can shame people to cover the needs of relatives in need. Such compulsions to give appear to precede (both psychologically and historically) the rationalizations of generous giving provided by religious traditions (Dresch 1998, 116). The compulsion to give that emerges in market transactions is similar to the relational pressures enforcing the obligation to cover the needs of relatives who have run out of money by giving them zakat or sadaqa.

This compulsion to give is taken up by references to Islamic concepts that are omnipresent in the markets of the city. A public culture of Islamic signifiers comprising stickers, signs, and greetings provides a wide ethical framework for zakat and market interactions alike. These signifiers directly describe the two models of zakat as passing on "God's wealth" and as making a "loan to God" in a divine system of bookkeeping. In market transactions, God's presence is similarly invoked as the Ultimate Provider of profit and as the Arbiter keeping track of transactions between human beings. The two images of God as Provider of wealth and as a Bookkeeper enable market sellers to pursue an ideal of piety by balancing tensions between the urge to be generous by giving things away for free and the necessity of making a living.

Nablus and Its Markets

At the time of my fieldwork in 2013 and 2014, the center of Nablus contained various street markets, or souks. They stretched out from the central square at the bottom of the valley within which the city of Nablus lies (fig. 5.1). In the old city, there were different souks for food (e.g., vegetables, fruits, meat, spices, and coffee), furniture, and clothing. Above the old city, residential areas expanded uphill with scattered small supermarkets, carpentries, locksmiths, and sewing workshops. Below the old city to the east of the central square was a gold market mainly selling jewelry commonly used for paying bridewealth. To the west of the central square, the city had been growing with the addition of large new commercial buildings, some that were still under construction and others that started to be partly filled with small shops and offices.[2]

This chapter focuses mainly on the markets in and around the old city. Two long streets cut through the old city from west to east. Sections of them were covered with steel constructions to protect the shops and the carts (*basṭa*) in the market from the summer heat or the winter rains. As one moved eastbound through the old city, prices decreased and the markets became more popular. At the eastern end of the old city, there was a large secondhand market that primarily offered goods no longer used in Israel and its settlements: clothes, electronic household devices, worn-out shoes, suitcases, and similar items. The

Figure 5.1. Central Square in Nablus at the entrance to the old city. © Jonas Opperskalski

refugee camps at the east end of the city (Balata and Askar) had small markets of their own. From the two central axes, side alleys led off into semiprivate residential areas called *ḥūj* (pl. *aḥwāj*). Inside these residential areas, it was not uncommon for traders to park small market carts overnight on a street corner with the agricultural products for the next day's sale, covered by a wet towel to keep them fresh.

Market fluctuations followed various daily, weekly, monthly, and annual rhythms. During the day, the old city markets were crowded. At nightfall, however, the shops were closed with metal gates and quickly deserted.[3] On Thursdays, the food markets became busy because families living in the city did most of their shopping for the food they cooked for the lunch after the midday prayer on Friday when all the mosques were full of people. The prices were quite high during the day on Thursdays before dropping in the late afternoon, as traders were keen to get rid of their perishable agricultural goods before Friday, when market activity stopped entirely in the morning and only sporadically resumed in the hours after the midday prayer and mosque sermons had ended. The markets were fully animated again on Saturday, when Palestinians living in Israel came to town to escape the closures of the Jewish Sabbath and take advantage of cheaper prices in Nablus. Visitors came in their cars and bought goods such as clothes, tahini (which is ground in some of the remaining Nablus factories), and olive oil, all of which cost much less in Nablus than anywhere in Israel.

Most importantly, sales in the markets depended on the monthly salary payments of the Palestinian Authority to its public sector employees (police officers, teachers, etc.), which a large number of households relied on. To carry out these payments, however, the Palestinian Authority relied on tax transfers from the Israeli authorities. These tax transfers were frequently withheld for political purposes, creating delays. At such times, the merchants in Nablus waited until the Palestinian Authority salaries descended on the city.

Finally, market fluctuations in Nablus also followed the rhythm of the Islamic calendar and its celebrations. Ramadan especially was expected to heat up the market. On this occasion, people are expected to spend more money and to give zakat to increase the intensity of the flow of wealth in a way that benefits the entire population. The month of Ramadan during my fieldwork, however, was overshadowed by a war between Israel and the Gaza Strip that partly stalled the flow of wealth, as described in chapter 1. People often described the souk as if it were a being with certain qualities. At times, the market was said to be hot (*ḥāmma*) or on fire (*nār*) to indicate that people were buying a lot and that prices were high. The analogy between business and fire was recurrent. For selling something over its price, the expression "burning them [the customers] in the price [*ḥarraqa-hum bi al-si'r*]" was occasionally used. In times of low turnover, merchants said that the market was sleeping (*nā'imah*), that there was no movement (*fish ḥaraka*), or that the market was *rā'iqa*, meaning calm or clear. According to a Greco-Arabist colleague, the word *rā'iq* is perhaps derived from the word *ruwāq* (a corridor of columns), which was used in the Abbasid period to translate the name of the philosophical school of the Stoics (*al-ruwāqiyūn*) into Arabic. Nowadays, "stoic calm," when applied to qualify the situation of the market, simply means "no business."

Shame in Market Transactions

Certain behavior in the market is classified as being shameful (*'ayb*). Consider the following example of a boy being admonished by his father. A little boy entered a fruit-juice shop all by himself and ordered the biggest and most expensive fruit cocktail with ice cream and a nut topping. When the cocktail was ready, the boy took a five-shekel coin out of his pocket and put it on the counter. The real price of the drink was eight shekels. The boy claimed not to have been aware of this. The shopkeeper smiled at this ruse and silently took the coin. The boy left with the cocktail in his hand. A few moments later, his father pulled him back into the shop. The father apologized dramatically to the shopkeeper for his boy's behavior and put another five-shekel coin on the counter. The shopkeeper vehemently refused to accept it, as it would have amounted to more than the real price. Finally, the father changed his tactics and put three one-shekel coins on the counter. The seller stated that this was not necessary at all and refused to pick them up from the counter. As this back-and-forth went on, the father simultaneously rebuked his son, repeatedly making it clear to him that what he had done was unacceptable. Finally, the father left the coins on the counter and walked out. In this situation, the father taught his son that taking something without paying its full price was shameful and introduced him to the implications that taking things has for a person's self-presentation.

In another situation, a market seller disciplined me after I refused to take herbs that he offered me for free. He grabbed my arm, pulled me close to him, and said, "This is shameful, man. Take these herbs!" This highlights how the issue of shame does not contain itself to dealings with people without means and gifts of zakat and sadaqa. Any gesture in the market that suggests neediness, whether on the side of the seller or on the side of the buyer, can trigger such accusations of shamefulness.

In the markets of Nablus, the shamefulness of signs of need is a recurrent theme because of people's awareness that their gestures and dealings are exposed to the observation and judgment of others. Let me provide a few examples of encounters where anxieties about the visibility of need disrupted the expected and mundane procedure of selling something. One day, I entered a little restaurant next to the roundabout with one of my friends from the group of textile workers I frequently spent time with. We ordered grilled meat sandwiches. The restaurant owner was an elderly man and an extended relative on the young man's mother's side. After serving him a sandwich and a can of soda, the restaurant owner said, "I am not taking from you." My friend put coins on the counter, then swiftly left the shop, ignoring the protestations of his relative. When we were both outside, he told me, "I do not like taking things from people for free." My friend was generally very mindful of how his transactions could affect his standing and reputation. According to my interpretation, the restaurant owner did not want to appear to be needy by taking money from a relative, while my friend did not want me to see him taking something for free and thereby displaying a sign of need, which would have compromised his autonomy.

Consider a similar scene that occurred on a cold winter morning. I was waiting in line in front of a small cart from which a young man was selling hot drinks on the central square of Nablus. Two other young men in front of me ordered coffee. When one of them took out his wallet to pay, the street vendor said, "I am not taking from you." The customer did not respond to this, and as he turned to leave, he put a five-shekel coin (covering the cost of two cups of coffee) on the cart next to the water tank and uttered a wish that God may give the vendor good health. Then the two young men took off with the paper cups in their hands. The vendor picked up the coin and ran after them. When he reached the man who had put the coin on his cart, the vendor tried to stuff it into one of the side pockets of the man's pants. The attempt failed, and the coin fell onto the pavement. The vendor picked the piece up once more and seemed ready to use physical force to make the young man accept the money. This customer started to worry that, if he continued to resist, the coffee might end up being spilled all over his clothes. He stopped moving and allowed the vendor to put the coin into one of his pockets. Only then did the situation calm down.

Discussing these kinds of events with people after they occurred is very difficult. Questions about the reasons people might have for acting in such a way can be perceived as inappropriate. After all, a person's answers could be used to taint his or her reputation. I strongly suspect, however, that the situation involving the coffee vendor and the customer escalated because so many people were there to witness the scene and both sides feared to be publicly seen as taking something inappropriately and thereby exposing a sign of need. Throughout my fieldwork, I witnessed a considerable number of similar interactions, often between young men. When a seller refused payment by saying "I am not taking from you," the market transaction swiftly turned into a gift-giving situation. It is possible to turn a sale into a gift but almost impossible to then reframe the interaction as a market exchange. The buyer's refusal of the gift (of receiving food or other goods for free) and insistence on paying made the money a gift to the seller. Because such situations cannot be reframed as market transactions, one side of the transaction will end up as the recipient of a gift. Which side turns out to be the recipient depends on how far each side is willing to go in creating a scene and attracting even more people's attention.

Such competitions in the public sphere over who is giving and who is taking also emerge between women. I witnessed one scene in public where two women confronted one another in such a competition. On an evening in November, the last passenger to get on a collective taxi (a Ford bus) leaving Ramallah heading to Nablus was an old woman. As the bus was leaving the building where the taxis were gathering, a younger woman standing on the street corner halted the bus and told the driver that she wanted to pay the ticket for the woman who had just boarded. When she heard this, the old woman protested loudly and told the driver, "Don't take [anything] from her [*tkhudhish min-hā*]!" The driver first hesitated and then accepted the payment from the woman looking into the window. She told him something that the others could not hear. The woman in the back of the Ford shouted at the other women, "Why did you bother yourself [*layh ghallabtī ḥāl-ek*]?" The driver turned to her and said, "Come on, extend your soul [*yalla ṭawwilī rūḥ-ek*]!" The male driver thus cut the confrontation short by asking the recipient of the gift for magnanimity and silence. This put an end to the exchange, and we drove off into the night toward Nablus. This scene suggests that the dynamics around gift giving and receiving at play in interactions between women are similar to those among men.

People in Nablus told me stories indicating that such small competitions resulting from gifts challenging someone's autonomy could escalate. One of my neighbors explained to me that when a gift gives rise to concerns over honor (*sharaf*), it often leads to far-reaching consequences. He told me the story of one of his ancestors, who lived in Nablus a few generations ago and owned a lot of land. One day, a friend of his invited him for lunch and slaughtered a sheep for him. The next day, the man went up to the man who had fed him and offered him an entire hill near Nablus as a countergift. The narrator of this story claimed that such practices of lavish, uncalculated giving were common in the past. For a similar story from Lebanon about a man giving away an olive grove for an orange because of "preferring glory (*majd*) to material substance, name to reason, and the grand gesture to personal interest," see Gilsenan (1996, 115–116). Returning to the market, we shall now explore how this compulsion to give is taken up in Islamic public culture in Nablus in an echo of the two models of zakat highlighting God's role as Provider of wealth and as Bookkeeper, respectively.

The Triad of Zakat Applied to Market Transactions

In the markets of Nablus, an Islamic public culture manifests itself on posters and stickers that contain concepts framing the transactions and the element of giving therein that I have identified above. These concepts directly map onto the two models of zakat discussed in this book. Rather than a triad between a giver of zakat, a recipient, and God, we are confronted with a triad of market seller, customer, and God. As in zakat, God is ascribed two different roles: the Ultimate Provider of wealth (the model of zakat as an "obligation to pass on God's wealth") and the Bookkeeper (the model of zakat as a "loan to God").

God as Ultimate Provider

As Ultimate Provider, God is assumed to be the origin of all wealth circulating through the market. In the Islamic tradition, the flow of money and material goods through society is said to emanate from God (Hallaq 2009, 296; Dresch 1998, 114). His provision is known as *rizq*, meaning both profit from legitimate trade and material sustenance or livelihood. *Rizq* is not only what people receive through gifts but also the money they earn, what they purchase in the market, and what they consume every day. In the context of markets, *rizq* is the material wealth bestowed on you through honest trade. In a more general sense, however, *rizq* is also the material produce provided by God that sustains human bodies. A vegetable seller who used to give me vegetables for free to eat on the spot as part of a long-term project of converting me to Islam explained to me that it is God alone that sustains us—not only spiritually but also materially: "As long as food and money flow to you, you live. When God stops this provision, you die. In this case, you might only get your *rizq* while you are in the grave or in paradise." He seemed to suggest that the vegetables he gave me were actually from God, a divine provision sustaining my body and health.

As explained in the second model of zakat in the introduction, a person's *rizq* does not result from a logic of calculation but is an expression of God's generosity. My interlocutors repeatedly taught me that the amount of *rizq* a person will receive in his or her life is a secret (*sirr*). An old man explained this to me in the following way: "It is impossible to know your future *rizq*. You need to strain yourself [*tshidd ḥāl-ak*] without seeking to know what you will get in return."[4] This suggests that one should have faith and rely on God while also trying to generate income for oneself and one's relatives. The relationship between the wealth a person obtains in this world and his or her ethical conduct inevitably remains a matter of guesswork. What if one's *rizq* is not flowing? According to my interlocutors, it could be delayed as part of a test of faith. On the other hand, there is always the danger that other people could interpret somebody's lack of *rizq* as a sign that God has withdrawn His sustenance to sanction presumed immoral behavior. This echoes the ambivalence, discussed with a view to zakat transactions, between the image of people struck by poverty as virtuous and close to God and their depiction as immoral.

What if one's *rizq* is flowing abundantly? Wealthy merchants often put up signs mentioning *rizq* near the counter, where customers pay for goods. They show, for instance, lists of things that one can do to gain *rizq*. In an expensive food shop in Nablus, a large poster behind the counter listed the "keys of *rizq*"—pious acts or states of mind that increase a person's *rizq* according to verses from the Quran: fearing God, seeking forgiveness and repentance, relying on God, spending wealth in the way of God, thanking God, marrying, giving up sins, aligning oneself with God's religion, and acting in obedience. Other posters spread across different shops in the city displayed invocations of

God to open the flow of His provision: "Invocation of *rizq*: Oh God! If my *rizq* is in heaven, make it come down. And if it is in the earth, make it emerge. And if it is hard, make it easy. And if it is illicit, purify it. And if it is far away, bring it closer. And if it is little, multiply it. And if it is a lot, bless it for me and turn it into a support for obeying and satisfying you in the reality [*bi-ḥaqq*] of your appearance, your brightness, your beauty, and your glory."

Such posters put up in stores have two performative functions. They express the merchant's commitment to Islamic piety and generosity while also legitimating financial success and the pursuit of profit as long as it is embedded within Islamic ethical commitments to the community. With such posters, the owners communicate that their store is part of a moral community (Elyachar 2005, 164). This implies that they are generous, give zakat and sadaqa, and refrain from asking their customers for unfair prices. In their general transactions, they stick to the rightful share (*ḥaqq*). In fact, the word *ḥaqq* is used for price in colloquial Arabic. Asking for the cost of a good, people say, "How much is its *ḥaqq*?" While God provides all wealth and people merely channel it, the notion of the just price brings calculated reasoning into play, which brings us to the other model for thinking about the triad between seller, customer, and God.

God as Bookkeeper Overseeing Transactions

Divine bookkeeping complements the concept of divine provision in Islamic public culture. My interlocutors told me that every person has two angels on his or her shoulders. The angel on the right registers the good deeds (*ḥasanāt*); the angel on the left, the bad deeds (*sayyi'āt*). From his or her divine account, a person will be recompensed in this life, in the period between death and Judgment Day, or in paradise. People emphasized that it is impossible for humans to know any details about this angelic accounting of loans and rewards since it belongs to the domain of "hidden things" (*umūr al-ghaybiyya*). Even if divine accounting takes place in an invisible field that largely eludes human perception and understanding, the image of God's bookkeeping encourages people to do good deeds as a means of gaining points in their own divine account.

Divine bookkeeping spans every sphere of human activity. It includes acts of worship (*'ibādāt*) and social interactions (*mu'āmalāt*). In a central mosque next to a water dispenser, a large poster provides a visual image of good deeds as coins next to a bag of money (fig. 5.2). Behind it, clouds open onto blue sky in allusion to people's transition to the Hereafter. The following text frames the image: "The inheritance of the Prophet (peace and blessings be upon him): [A list of deeds bringing forth] the reward [*thawab*] of virtuous work [*al-'aml al-ṣāliḥ*]. The lucrative trade with God does not perish." Golden coins in the image carry the words *ablution, fasting*, and *prayer*. The word *inheritance* refers to the many *ḥadīth* indicating how people can gain divine reward. To the right and to the left of the central image are long lists of deeds that are said to increase one's account with God—similar to the list of things one can do to gain *rizq* discussed earlier.

While this poster foregrounds acts of worship for gaining reward, the concept of divine bookkeeping makes it possible to think of one's interactions with others as a way of working on one's own salvation.[5] The way people do business, for instance, is assumed to directly affect divine bookkeeping. Traders who are being stingy, cheating, or ripping people off with exaggerated prices have to fear that good deeds will be deducted from their accounts on Judgment Day. These deeds would then be added to the accounts of the people whom the traders deprived of their rightful share. People who are ripped off in a transaction but end up indirectly increasing their recompense in the Hereafter in such a way are called the owners of the rightful share (*aṣḥāb al-ḥaqq*). In this sense, the concept of divine bookkeeping allows people to make the ethical aspects related to the flow of wealth more transparent. In a certain sense, bookkeeping establishes a direct connection between dealings in this world and the accounting that occurs in the Other World or the Hereafter.

According to a young man working in a car repair shop, deceased persons' financial debts in this world risk incurring deductions from their accounts in the system of divine bookkeeping. Consequently, family members (especially in the old city of Nablus) would ask around whether the deceased person had open debts. Creditors, if there were any, would either ask for their rightful share (*ḥaqq*) or free the deceased person and his family from the obligation of paying it back by saying, "God forgive him or her [*allah ysāmiḥ-hu/hā*]." If the creditor insisted on being paid, the relatives of the deceased would seek to gather the sum and cover the debt on his or her behalf. This is because relatives fear that debt would negatively affect the well-being of a deceased person in the grave and possibly lower his or her chance of entering paradise. If the relatives failed to pay back the open debt, God's bookkeepers might deduct good deeds from the account of the deceased and transfer them to the account of the creditor—especially when the debtor did not have the intention (*niyya*) to pay back the debt, something that only God can know. Notice that this shifting of good deeds from one account to another also works in the other direction: when a creditor died whose debtor had no intention of paying back what he or she owed, the debt was said to turn into betrayal and theft, which are classified as severely bad deeds (*sayi'āt*).

Figure 5.2. A fragment of a poster in a mosque in central Nablus containing extensive lists of *ḥadīth* connecting various pious practices to the gaining of divine reward in the Hereafter. © Jonas Opperskalski

Gifts to others can increase the points in one's own account. If, at the end of a Ramadan day, one woman feeds another woman who has been fasting, the good deeds that the woman receiving food has gained for fasting are assumed to be also written down in the account of the giver. In other words, the points resulting from one person's fasting for the period of one day is registered twice as a result of this gift of food. This again strongly echoes the model of zakat in which God acts as Bookkeeper, meticulously accounting for anything that is given. Such calculative framings of giving raise the question of how the tension between uncalculated generosity underpinned by divine provision and the calculating spirit running through divine bookkeeping is dealt with in Islamic public culture in Nablus.

The Tensions between Generous Giving and Calculated Bookkeeping

Giving often springs from a compulsion to be generous and from a desire to appear to be a channel of God's provision. Thus, the Islamic public culture in Nablus takes up the compulsion to be generous. At the same time, the concept of divine bookkeeping enables calculative moral reasoning about acts of giving and market transactions. Explaining this tension between calculation and uncalculated generosity, Mittermaier (2013) distinguishes between an economy of reward (*thawāb*) and an economy of blessing (*baraka*), which in my interpretation maps onto the complementary models of God as Bookkeeper and as Ultimate Provider and Sustainer. The economy of reward gives rise to the image of "trading with God" and gaining "points." The economy of blessing, however, is organized according to a logic of (ultimately abundant) uncalculated divine generosity. Mittermaier's interlocutors noted that divine blessing and the good (*al-khayr*)—mostly used in the sense of doing good to others—can disrupt the "logic of the calculator" (2013, 276, 284, 286). In fact, "single decisive acts" (284), such as those transmitted in a famous *ḥadīth* where a prostitute uses her shoe to give water to a dog that is about to die from thirst, can suspend calculation. According to the *ḥadīth*, God saved the prostitute from hell solely on the basis of this one decisive deed.

In Nablus, posters and stickers recall the importance of seemingly small acts and virtues that undo the "logic of the calculator." A sticker in a mosque in central Nablus suggests that a state of mind devoted to the "extolment and praise to God ... fills the scale" on Judgment Day with divine merit (fig. 5.3). The picture shows a scale that carries planet Earth in one bowl, which is outweighed by the content of the other bowl: the phrase "extolment and praise to God." This minor expression is cast as weighing heavier than all worldly affairs combined. Pronouncing it often and cultivating gratitude toward God is thus framed as a decisive act disrupting calculated measuring in the divine accounting of good deeds.

Another example of a "decisive" act is to embody the virtue of "relying on God" (*tawakkul*) in one's daily business. At several entrances to the souks of central Nablus, posters with the following text hung over market alleys as people passed underneath:

> Invocation before entering the souk: ... [Regarding] those who entered the souk and said, "There is no deity except for God alone and nothing equals

Figure 5.3. A sticker found on a water tank in a mosque in central Nablus. © Author

Him [*lā sharīka la-hu*]. His is the power [of owning] [*la-hu al-mulk*] and His is the praise. He gives life and death. . . ." God will register on their behalf thousands and thousands of good deeds and eradicate on their behalf thousands and thousands of bad deeds and raise them thousands and thousands of levels and build them a house in paradise.

Reliance on God cannot be measured or quantified. It breaks calculation apart by bringing forth excessive amounts ("thousands and thousands") of entries of good deeds in God's books. The term *tawakkul* literally means to entrust God with one's own affairs. It defines a state of alertness and faith—a readiness to accept God's will with a view to future events. In other words, it is the absence of worries and second thoughts about the uncertainties of the future. On the other hand, bookkeeping is not to be taken all too seriously. My interlocutors stated that no one would enter paradise because of their good deeds (or points) alone; all depended solely on God's mercy.[6] Such readings foreground the role of God as Ultimate Provider and Sustainer over his role as Bookkeeper.

Pious Merchants

As an Islamic virtue, *tawakkul* unfolds in the triad of God and the human parties to a transaction. Trusting a person one is doing business with is an expression of one's reliance on God. As in relations between givers and receivers of zakat, good relations among sellers and customers require openness to the unpredictable and attention to others. Piety extends to the readiness to have faith in a person one is doing business with or, indeed, to have faith that one's relatives or neighbors will provide food if one cannot do so oneself. Unlike in the Christian tradition, where money can be viewed as a source of moral danger and the merchant is often a morally dubious figure (Le Goff 1990), being an honest trader is considered a considerable ethical achievement, and Islamic scholars even celebrate certain merchants as exemplars of piety (Graeber 2011, 291).[7] According to one saying of the Prophet often cited by my interlocutors, the honest trader (*al-tājir al-ṣadūq*) will be gathered on Judgment Day together with the prophets, the honest people (*ṣādiqīn*), and the martyrs. Merchants in Nablus seeking to cultivate a reputation for piety nevertheless remain challenged by the tension between calculated and uncalculated generosity. This is revealed in the stickers placed around their stores.

A merchant is closely tied to the space of his or her store. The shop can be seen as an allegory for the self of its keeper, as it represents his or her place on earth. Many merchants spend decades in their shops. The shop of a merchant, his or her "place" (*maḥall*), is embedded in social interactions that are ethically judged by the wider community. Merchants index their commitment to Islam by means of stickers inside and outside their places. Many shop stickers remind people to pray: "The Prophet longs to be prayed for!" or "Why don't you pray?" followed by a list of the benefits of prayer, one of which is that it links the self to God. This suggests that certain merchants fulfill the Islamic duty to laterally discipline others in their surroundings by advising them to pray.

Another extremely widespread sticker states, "God has willed it [*mā shā' allah*]!" Like the stickers mentioning *rizq* discussed above, the expression "God has willed it" deflects envy in the eyes of others and legitimates making a profit. This echoes Elyachar's (2005) ethnography of a neighborhood full of car repair shops in Cairo. The owners of a financially successful shop tended to use Islamic posters that mentioned *rizq* to fend off envy and the evil eye, stating: "God willing. God provides [material wealth] to whom he wants (*allah yarzuqu man yashā'*)" (163). Such signs, according to Elyachar, represent attempts to protect shopkeepers from envious competitors who might try to draw them into moral scandals or bring about misfortune—for instance, by setting a workshop on fire in what would seem to be an extreme form of lateral disciplining. Although I did not come across similar stories in Nablus, Elyachar's point that such signs signal a merchant's commitment to social obligations as framed by Islamic public culture applies to Nablus as well.

The Disciplining Effects of Rizq

The discourse of divine provision has a disciplinary effect on merchants as it implies compliance with a number of ethical principles. First, it suggests that one does not pursue income from illegitimate sources. Those through whose hands divine provision flows are entitled to profit from it, as long as they avoid trading illicit goods and do not engage in usury. According to Ahmed Sharaf, the sheikh on the Nablus Zakat Committee introduced in chapter 2, *rizq* is the wealth accumulated according to the principles laid out in the Islamic tradition regarding the induction of wealth (*jalb al-māl*) and its expenditure (*infāq al-māl*). The *rizq* is, therefore, by definition licit (*ḥalāl*) and cannot be illicit (*ḥarām*). The opposite of *rizq*, following this view, is illicit gain (*kasb ḥarām*) or illicit tradable wealth (*māl ḥarām*). The religiously committed traders among my interlocutors were concerned about keeping their material and financial possessions licit (*ḥalāl*), which primarily meant not dealing with illicit substances, such as alcohol, drugs, or pork. A few pious merchants even counted cigarettes as illicit goods and refrained from selling them, fully conscious of the fact that they were missing out on considerable profit from such sales. On the other hand, they did not want to risk tainting their pious reputations. Moreover, many merchants tried to keep their wealth pure from usury (*ribā*). What this meant in practice was not always very clear. Even traders who attended classes taught in mosques on how Islamic concepts can shape the everyday life of merchants were not always sure to what extent it was possible to take up a loan from an Islamic bank, given that the Islamic banks are linked to the global "usurious" system. Some went as far as to argue that one drop of usury among one's wealth [*māl*] would pollute the ritual purity [*ṭahāra*] of one's entire body and thereby invalidates one's prayers.

Second, the notion of *rizq* implies an obligation for merchants to share information about the market openly with customers. A spice merchant told me that the idea that *rizq is in the hand of God* obliges pious traders to lead customers to other shops if they do not carry the requested products in their own stores. Abiding with this obligation is hailed as a sign of piety, even though merchants risk losing customers to another trader.

Third, the notion of divine provision puts pious merchants under the moral obligation to pass parts of it on for free by giving it away to people in need as zakat or sadaqa. Consider the following statement I heard about a highly successful shop: A store selling sweets, chips, and cold sodas had been thriving for months, offering steadily more goods for sale. As the goods no longer fit into the small space, they were held for sale in the narrow market alley, into which they bulged out on both sides of the door. When I talked to the owner of a small fruit shop situated about ten meters from this place, he pointed to his wealthy neighbor with admiration and explained, "His business over there is going extremely well because he has been spending a lot for the sake of the poor and the needy. When you give discreetly and then forget about it, God gives to you." With this statement, the owner of the fruit shop dispersed any suggestion that he might feel envy toward his neighbor. On the other hand, he seemed to suggest not only that the neighbor had been giving to people in need but also that he *should* be giving. This kind of talk in the city underpins a subtle pressure on successful merchants to support people in need.

Leniency toward people in need and small gestures of generosity, such as offering gifts of food to people considered helpless, are thus part of everyday life for pious merchants. Consider the following example of a sandwich place on a noisy road in the center of Nablus (outside the old city). Ahmed, the owner, cared about a pious reputation. Once, a bearded old man in old clothes stepped into Ahmed's shop. He murmured Islamic greetings and blessings and waited to be given a sandwich for free. Then he added, "We are all God's guests"—reminding those who were present that God is the source of all material wealth. After Ahmed had given him a sandwich, he disappeared into the stream of people on the sidewalk. Ahmed would offer the space of the shop for people to pray or relax. He often invited people from the neighborhood to sit down on a chair in the back of his shop and poured them a cup of tea. Occasionally, a police officer would walk into the shop and say a few words of greeting. After washing hands, arms, face, and neck with water from a sink in the back of the shop, the officer would lay out a small carpet and pray behind a large refrigerator containing beverages. Ahmed sought to construct the space of his shop as welcoming and as a channel of the flow of divine provision providing food to those in need. In this sense, the notion of *rizq* encourages or disciplines pious shopkeepers to be lenient and generous in offering their goods as well as their space to others.

The Disciplining Effects of Divine Bookkeeping

Divine bookkeeping also has a disciplinary effect on small merchants. It underpins the everyday giving of merchants, such as when they give to care for their deceased father who ran their shop before them. Ahmed, for instance, offered water to travelers for free to increase the good deeds of his father in his grave. It was the wish of Ahmed's father before he died to install this drinking fountain as a form of flowing alms (*ṣadaqa jāriya*). The water tank under the roof of Ahmed's shop fed a tap over a little sink on a wall out in the street. The tap was removable. Ahmed would put it there during the day so the people passing in the street could drink from it. At night, he removed the tap to prevent people from emptying the tank. He regularly filled the tank with water that was paid for by the income of the shop. Above the sink, the following words, painted black, had been carved into a light-gray stone plate: "And we made from water every living thing [Quran 21, 30]. Water of the path [*mā' al-sabīl*]. Only for drinking." Ahmed told me that, regardless of social class, every time a person drank from the fountain, good deeds were registered on behalf of his deceased father, even though he was already in his grave, waiting for Judgment Day. While increasing the points of the deceased man, the water was also viewed as an expression of God's generous provision slaking the thirst of travelers who visited Nablus.

The calculative logic of divine bookkeeping, suggesting that a merchant asking for unfair prices risks a deduction of good deeds from his Godly account, can have a disciplinary effect causing merchants not to charge too much. On the other hand, it can also prevent sellers from undercutting what is commonly agreed to be a fair price. I witnessed a discussion among food merchants about a merchant who was buying huge quantities of bottled soft drinks and then selling them under the commonly accepted price. This led to an organized intervention whereby other merchants put pressure on this man to make him raise the price again. In conclusion, the conceptions of God as both the origin of uncalculated provision and the meticulous Bookkeeper overseeing transactions are resources people can tap into to discipline one another in market activities. Nevertheless, tensions sometimes arise between traders and customers around the competing ethic of generosity and the necessity of making a living, discussed next.

Navigating Tensions among Calculation, Generous Giving, and Reliance on God

Market sellers and merchants who serve people considered helpless for free are lauded for their generosity and piety, earning them respect. Therefore, people presenting themselves as helpless can actively extract food or drinks by walking into shops and asking for something. I witnessed several occasions where this worked out well for those presenting themselves as helpless in the sense of not shying away from openly exposing their material want. Occasionally, however, shopkeepers need to redraw the boundaries between their own leniency in transactions and their commercial interest. Early in the morning on a winter day, I waited in line in a small food store. Two men in worn-out clothes entered and started picking up small bags of chips. They waved them in the air to gain the shopkeeper's attention. With the bag of chips in his hand, one of them looked straight into the shopkeeper's eyes, apparently expecting a gesture of agreement that he could take it without paying. The seller, however, refused to make such a sign. Instead, he asked his customers to excuse him for a moment and came out from behind the counter. He walked up to the two downtrodden men and rubbed his fingers in front of their faces, saying, "I need to see some shekels!" One of the men said that their pockets were empty. They put back the chips, and then they both walked out of the shop. The shopkeeper returned to his place behind the counter and continued serving customers. This example points out the limits sellers face in enacting their shops as channels of divine generosity and provision.

On the other hand, sometimes merchants with a reputation of piety are accused of being misers and skinflints. When it comes to the bad qualities a trader can be known for, greed (*bukhl*) appears to be the worst, next to cheating and dishonesty, and it gives rise to the most ridiculing through gossip. People tended to lower their voice when conveying stories about merchants or shopkeepers with a pious reputation who would charge money for minor services.

Many shopkeepers put up signs to prevent too many requests from customers wishing to take things for free or on credit and then neglect paying it back. Many shopkeepers in Nablus had grown reluctant to provide vital goods on credit to people who were unable to pay. Signs saying "no credit" were widespread in shops. One of the signs with such a message showed a hundred-dollar bill (fig. 5.4). Next to the picture of Benjamin Franklin, the following Arabic text was inserted: "Debt is forbidden, blaming [the shopkeeper] is suspended, and divine provision depends on God [*wa al-rizq 'alā allah*]. Please do not open a discussion on this subject." According to the owner of the shop, this sign helped to keep people from making a scene (*iḥrāj*). Merchants did not want to provide goods to people on credit because they knew that such debts were seldom paid.

In Nablus, putting up dollar signs (with or without Arabic text added to them) was quite common. Even shopkeepers with a reputation for piety would do so. Rather than seeing in the dollar a symbol of usury, they told me that they "like the dollar." To them, the dollar seemed to symbolize the profit that comes from market transactions, echoing the conception of *rizq*. The reference to the US dollar implies a more universal level of value than the Israeli shekel, which is used for most transactions in the occupied Palestinian territories. The Arabic

Figure 5.4. A dollar-bill sign put up in shops in Nablus with Arabic text stating that one cannot buy things on credit and that the flow of wealth is in God's hands. © Author

text in the sign shown here, on the other hand, brings the universalism of the dollar into relation with the universal appeal of Islam. In this context, divine provision (*rizq*) is explicitly used for disentangling the merchant from relational pressures to pass part of God's wealth on to others. Here, those without money are reminded that the wealth of the affluent has been bestowed on them by God and that this should be respected. In this context, the disciplinary effects of *rizq* work the other way around. Rather than disciplining the merchant into giving, *rizq* legitimizes the pursuit of profit in the market and frames it as an endeavor that is aligned with the Islamic tradition.

Through their interactions and transactions with others, merchants and shopkeepers in Nablus balance concerns for their own financial success, piety, the well-being of relatives in their graves, self-esteem, honor, and shame. A small poster put up at the counter of an old city café made the need to negotiate such sometimes-competing values in market transactions explicit:

> Oh Lord,
> If you give me tradable wealth [*māl*], do not take away my happiness.
> If you give me strength, do not take away my reason [or ability of self-control].
> If you give me eminence [*jāh*], do not take away my modesty [*tawāḍuʿ*].
> If you give me modesty, do not take away my self-esteem [*ʿizza*].
> If you give me influence, do not take away my being forgiven [*ʿafū*].

Customers reading this sign gain an insight into the inner speech of the owner of the shop, who publicly displays his efforts at keeping wealth, strength, and honor (eminence) in balance with virtues associated with Muslim piety. This highlights how dealings in the market are deeply connected with different ethical concerns. Engaging in such dealings, many merchants in Nablus display their piety to others through signs, ethical commitments, and gestures of leniency and generosity toward people who expose their need.[8]

The two models of God as Provider and as Bookkeeper invoked in market transactions are complementary. They allow for different forms of disciplining in the marketplace and directly connect transactions with God and the Hereafter or the Other World. The disciplinary force partly arises from the fact that people constantly remind one another about the possibility of divine justice underpinning transactions in the market. God plays the role of the fundamental arbiter, witness, and judge in the course of mundane market transactions between people (see also Schielke 2018, 5). While divine bookkeeping and divine provision cannot be fully grasped by humans, the Hereafter and the invisible or "hidden things" continuously manifest themselves in this world. The next chapter turns to situate people's relation with the Other World in the context of Israeli military occupation and a political economy based on security clearances and far-reaching surveillance.

6

The Other World and the Occupation

The conceptualization of zakat as divine money connects the everyday lives of Palestinians with the partly invisible realm of the divine. Zakat as a manifestation of divine sustenance has gained even more symbolic value under conditions of political repression because it suggests that God is supporting Palestinian Muslims as they deal with the pressures of surviving occupation by a non-Muslim power. Throughout the time I was in the field, Palestinian business undertakings tended to be contingent on security clearances and a complex system of permits. This curtailed Palestinian economic development. In the face of Israeli settlement expansion around Nablus, remaining on the land and making a decent living was fraught with challenges and dilemmas for many inhabitants of the city. As discussed in the preceding chapters, institutionalized and informal zakat and sadaqa transfers from abroad and within the local community became important material resources. Such transactions enabled people to survive and remain steadfast in an occupied territory.[1]

This chapter examines the ways in which ideas about the Other World coexist with contemporary political and economic landscapes in Palestine (see also Mittermaier 2013, 278–279). It explores how people connect with the invisible world of God and the Hereafter as they confront the realities of Israeli occupation in their everyday lives. My ethnographic work in Nablus suggests that many Palestinian Muslims conceive of the Other World not merely as something yet to come after they die but as something continuously interwoven with the world of the living. This gives rise to a number of problems, however. How can one hold on to the idea that all wealth comes from God when an occupying power obviously controls economic activities in Palestine? How can one hold on to Muslim piety and the notions of justice that underpin it in a context where making a living often requires acquiescence to the occupation? I argue that divine bookkeeping and divine provision enable people to live ethical lives under conditions of political repression because they invoke an elusive Other World whose presence nonetheless shines through and manifests itself in this world. As such, ideas of divine bookkeeping and provision constitute resources for confronting the conditions created by the occupation.[2]

I first discuss some of the ways the invisible world manifests in the world of the living by providing an ethnographic account of funerals and gravesites in Nablus. Next, I turn to stories told in Nablus of past episodes of foreign rule and oppression that suggest that ultimate divine justice continues to manifest in the lives of Palestinians. Such stories about the manifestation of the Other World in this world expand the reach of Islamic public culture and its potential for lateral disciplining by establishing a minimal level of communal accountability in an otherwise opaque political landscape. After analyzing the limits of this lateral disciplining in addressing economic power relations, I explore problems arising from the need to make a living while also leading an ethical life under repressive political conditions. Finally, the material presented in this book is situated in the wider context of the contemporary Middle East.

Connections to the Other World

In Nablus, funerals are an important part of everyday life. Death is widely understood to be the beginning of a transition to another state of existence. Funerals are social events where this world and the Other World come into touch with each other in two ways. First, funerals are liminal moments when the body of the deceased transitions into the Other World. Second, funerals involve a number of transactions that are said to affect the account of good deeds of the deceased as well as the account of the people attending the funeral feasts. Thus, when a shopkeeper who has been a well-known personality in the city dies, the shop is closed for several days (sometimes weeks) and a handwritten sign that mentions divine bookkeeping and announces the dates of the funeral feasts is put on the closed gates of the store. The following is a representative example of such a sign:

> In the name of God, the Gracious and Compassionate
> "Every human being [*nafs*] is bound to taste death: but only on the Day of Resurrection will you be requited in full [*tuwaffūna ujūr-kum* (sg. *ajr*)] [for whatever you have done]." [Quran 3, 185]
> The place is closed
> Because of the death of its owner

[Name of the owner]
"We belong to God and to Him we are returning." [Quran 2, 156]
The prayer of the funeral will take place in the [name of the mosque]
The pilgrim [*ḥajj*, here used as a title] [name of the host—usually the son of the deceased] will accept condolences [*taʿāzī*] in his house
[Date; from this day onward, the house will be open for three days for men and for two days for women serving coffee, dates, and lunch in the afternoon]

Mourning is part of public life. Burial preparations and processions and funeral receptions are all points of contact between this world and the Other World. Before the burial procession, the relatives wash the body of the deceased to purify them. Then, after a joint prayer "over" (*ʿalā*) the deceased person in the mosque, a group of men carries the coffin to one of the city's cemeteries. Walking behind coffins through the city is another part of Islamic ethical interactions (*muʿāmalāt*). It is considered respectful to join processions and visit the family of the deceased.

Like zakat transactions, the interactions surrounding funerals connect people to the Other World by invoking God as the Provider and Sustainer of people beyond their death and as the Bookkeeper who encourages relatives to give on behalf of the dead and thereby increase the good deeds stored in their accounts. The following ethnographic accounts of two funerals—one for a Palestinian martyr and the other for a woman—that occurred on the same day in the Nablus cemetery convey a sense of how such contact points with the Other World unfold within the context of armed conflict and tense politics under military occupation.

One warm evening in March, I heard a voice from the loudspeakers from a mosque near my place. It announced the funeral of Palestinian martyrs to be held on the next day. The following morning, my neighbors told me that Israeli forces had returned the dead bodies of martyrs to their relatives in Nablus. The most prominent martyr (*shahīd*) among them was Mohammed Abd al-Rahim al-Hanbali, who held a high position in the armed wing of Hamas during the Second Intifada. Israeli soldiers had killed him during an arrest operation more than ten years earlier, on September 5, 2003, and then captured his dead body (Haaretz 2003). The funeral was held in 2013 because only then had an exchange deal been reached. Israelis and Palestinians commonly keep the corpses of their enemies so they can use them to later negotiate an exchange. Such deals sometimes combine the release of live prisoners with the return of the bodies of the deceased. People said that the aim of withholding dead bodies was to "burn the blood of their relatives." In such cases, relatives are unable to arrange for the appropriate rituals that ordinarily accompany the deceased persons to the grave. This gives rise to fears that the deceased may suffer during the transition into the Hereafter as a result. Against this background, the ability to bury Mohammed Abd al-Rahim was highly important to his relatives.

The day after I heard the announcement from the mosque, I went to visit some friends at the sewing shop. They informed me that the sister of one of the workers had unexpectedly passed away from heart failure the night before. The workers were getting ready to attend her burial and asked me whether I would like to go with them to the mosque and then follow the coffin to the cemetery. When I hesitated about accompanying them to the mosque, one of them asked whether it would be normal (*'ādī*) if I joined them. Another young man who was related to the deceased woman replied, "To the mosque? I don't know." I respected that and so stayed in the shop with two other workers, who said they would take me directly to the cemetery for the burial.

In the Cemetery

Two hours later, the two sewing workers and I walked to the Western Cemetery of Nablus, which stretches from the west end of the old city up the southern mountain. The graves are rectangular boxes made of white stone with tombstones at their ends. They stick out of the earth underneath a cypress grove. All the graves are aligned perpendicularly to the direction of prayer. According to my interlocutors, the dead bodies in the graves are placed lying on their right side so they will face southeast, the direction of Mecca. We entered the cemetery and climbed up a little hill, passing between different graves to wait for the funeral procession from the mosque to arrive at the cemetery. The earth under our feet was dark brown and a little damp. The sun's rays fell through the branches of the cypress trees. Small flowers blossomed between the graves, and the ground was covered with new shoots. The smell of the young plants and fresh earth filled the air.

While we were waiting for the woman's burial procession to arrive, Mohammed al-Hanbali's funeral ceremony began in the upper part of the cemetery. The organization of this burial had been subject to political tension. Palestinian Authority security forces had tried to arrange a nationalist ceremony with military honors and a public parade consisting of Palestinian security personnel. Hamas had refused to allow the PA to influence the funeral, however. I read in news reports that armed men from Hamas had attacked the ambulance used to transport the remains of the deceased man when it reached Nablus. Allegedly, they removed the body from the Palestinian flag within which the security forces had wrapped him, then rewrapped him in the green flag of the Islamic movement, on which the words "There is no deity except for God and Mohammed is God's Prophet" were written in white calligraphy.

Earlier, a procession of at least two hundred people had entered the graveyard through the entrance on the opposite side, about 150 meters away from where I stood with my textile worker friends. The men following the coffin waved posters carrying the image of Mohammed al-Hanbali and green flags that signaled their allegiance to Hamas. Dignified, elderly bearded men wearing long clothes and *kufiyas* entered the cemetery and slowly headed up the hill to join the burial ritual of the former fighter. My friends told me that these men were representatives of important families in Nablus. I then noticed Palestinian security forces taking pictures and videotaping the men heading for Mohammed al-Hanbali's funeral. I later saw that the streets surrounding the cemetery were full of police cars and uniformed Palestinian security forces carrying weapons. As I waited, I could hear speeches being delivered up the hill where the martyr was to be buried. Mohammed al-Hanbali's funeral illustrates how connections with the Other World link up with the reality of occupation, as in the exchange of bodies with Israeli authorities, the political contestations around the funeral processions, and the presence of security personnel and surveillance activities in the cemetery.

This atmosphere also cast a shadow on the woman's funeral I was attending. Unlike the martyred man, the body of the deceased woman was carried in a simple wooden coffin by ten men. When they arrived, we followed the procession to the spot where the woman was to be buried. We stood in concentric circles with about eighty men around the open grave. There was not a single woman in the entire cemetery that day. Four men held a yellow-brown blanket above the pit of the grave as other men lowered the body into the earth. Pearls of sweat formed on the foreheads of some of the men. In a rhythmic chorus, we began repeating the sentence "There is no deity except for God [*lā ilāha illā allah*]." The recitation stopped and was taken up again. One man leaned far into the pit of the grave, grieving his loss; other men held him as he bent down to the earth.

One of my friends suggested going to another part of the cemetery to visit the grave of his brother, who had been shot by an Israeli soldier as a teenager while he was throwing stones at Israeli forces invading one of the refugee camps. We stepped out of the group of men standing around the grave and picked up a broom and three plastic bottles from a little shack. My friend filled the bottles with water from a tap and gave some of them to me. At the grave of his brother, he sat down on a small bench, laid his hands on his thighs, and began to pray silently. When he finished his internal recitation of Quranic text, he lifted his cupped hands and brushed them over his face as if with water. I sat down next to him, and we remained in silence for a few moments. The grave was a lengthy box made of white stone standing on a little pedestal covered with tiles. We cleaned the tiles of dust and twigs. Once we finished cleaning, we took the bottles and watered small flowerpots on both sides of the grave. Finally, my friend poured water all over the white stone grave and used his hands to clean it carefully. He said to me, "People think that when you sprinkle water [on the grave], the dead person [inside] relaxes." On our way back to the lower exit of the cemetery, we realized that everyone had already left the grave of the deceased woman. We only met her husband, who was heading back to her grave, carrying a little booklet with verses from the Quran. He said that he wanted to sit at the grave and read the Quran over ('alā) his wife.

The sprinkling of water and the reciting of the Quran near graves illustrate how people continue to connect to the deceased. The dead are not assumed to have disappeared but to still be present in the grave waiting for Judgment Day. The Other World thus has a presence in this world that involves relationships of care for the dead. They are looked after in their graves, and transactions are made on their behalf to increase their divine accounts of good deeds. For example, regular payments of supererogatory alms (sadaqa) may be given by the living on behalf of deceased persons (as discussed in earlier chapters).

After we exited the cemetery, I saw that the male relatives of the deceased woman had lined up along the external graveyard wall under a tin roof. They were shaking the hands of men who had come to express their condolences. Joining my friend in the line, I was told to shake hands with all the relatives and console each of them by saying, "May God magnify your recompense ['azzam allah ajr-kum]." This statement invokes the divine bookkeeping that underpins the transactions taking place around funerals.

Transactions Surrounding Funerals

Around funerals, the flows of sadaqa intensify. It is common to give money, on behalf of deceased family members, to people in need who are present at the graveyard. Doing so is said to enhance the well-being of the deceased in the grave and increase their spiritual merit with a view to the Hereafter. The Arabic word for funeral hosting is 'azā'. In Nablus, an 'azā' takes place over the course of two days for a deceased woman or three days for a man. The family of the deceased person hosts neighbors and friends in a family divan or in a private home. Women and men remain strictly separate.

Everybody is invited to a lunch, mostly consisting of rice and meat, in the early afternoon. During the rest of the day, people serve black coffee and dates to visitors. Men sit on chairs and chat. In their aesthetic of abundance and their occasional feeding of entire neighborhoods, such funeral feasts invoke the image of divine provision. They are a gift to people in the vicinity enacted by an entire family (usually an agnatic kin group). Hosting and feeding hundreds of people from the surrounding area manifests an extended family's ability to give generously. One of my neighbors told me that families "like to give out food in order to show their appreciation of the person who has passed away [*biʿizzū ʿalā al-mayyit*]." He explained that most relatives and neighbors give money to the immediate family of the deceased so their women can cook the good food provided at funeral feasts.

The acts of giving surrounding funerals directly resonate with the principle of divine bookkeeping. In Nablus, funeral receptions are often called a "house of recompense" (*bayt ajr*), an allusion to God's accounting of everyone's good and bad deeds. My interlocutors told me that the giving of food and the payment of sadaqa surrounding funerals benefited the deceased person in the grave and facilitated his or her passage into the Hereafter. Moreover, attending a funeral feast is said to increase one's own good-deeds account. And, as on my exit from the cemetery, guests express their condolences to members of the extended family of the deceased by saying, "May God magnify your [plural form] recompense."

As a funeral reception extends throughout the day, an elderly man sometimes leads a prayer in the divan for those who missed the prayer in the mosque. I once heard an old man who was leading the prayer at such an occasion recite the following verses of the Quran (74, 44–46):

> They [the criminals] will say, "We were not of those who prayed,
> Nor did we use to feed the poor.
> And we used to enter into vain discourse with those who engaged [in it],
> And we used to deny the Day of Recompense
> Until there came to us the certainty."

These verses directly relate to the duty to give. They illustrate again how fragments of Islamic scriptures are continuously woven into public life in the city. The verses selected by the old man also connect giving to the human transition into the Other World.

Stories about God Sustaining the Virtuous

The Other World is also assumed to manifest itself in this world through God's power as a Sustainer and Provider. Islamic public culture in Nablus draws on stories that cast this divine system of sustenance as one of ultimate justice against the odds of foreign domination and political repression. The following stories that circulated in Nablus at the time of my fieldwork illustrate how God sustains the pious and virtuous or withdraws His sustenance from those who act immorally.

The Story of the Immovable Corpse

In the streets of Nablus, there are several shrines connected to the "graves of pious persons" (*maqām*, pl. *maqāmāt*).[3] Sufi circles meet inside or around these shrines and take care of them. The corpses of highly pious and virtuous personalities buried in these graves reportedly remain intact and manifest considerable material solidity. People in Nablus told me different versions of a story about one of these shrines. The green shrine, cuboid in shape, is situated at the margins of the ruins of an ancient Roman hippodrome not far from an area where real estate investors have recently constructed many commercial buildings (fig. 6.1).

Many of my interlocutors ascribed the grave to a renowned exemplar of moral behavior, the Islamic scholar Sufiyan al-Thawri (AD 716–778), who is said to be "among those who have achieved true piety [*min al-ṣāliḥūn*]."[4] Although the details of the stories told about his shrine vary according to the age of the storyteller, they all center on a common theme in which the body of the pious man in the grave either negatively affects non-Muslim foreign rulers (British or Israeli at various historical moments) who come into contact with it or becomes recalcitrant when they try to remove or disturb his grave.

One old man told me that the following version hearkens back to the British Mandate in Palestine: "In the 1920s, an English archaeologist and military man came to Nablus and started digging at the western end of the Roman hippodrome, right at the place the grave stands today. At that time, there was nothing indicating the presence of the grave of a pious man. The Englishman was digging up the earth when he felt a sudden strike in his back and he could not move any more. People took him to the hospital, where he died the next day. This is from God!" This account suggests that in spite of nascent non-Muslim rule over the city, God's justice manifested itself by hindering British power from dislodging the corpse of a pious Muslim in a grave.

A group of men running a grocery store next to the grave situated another version of the story in the period of early Israeli rule over the West Bank:

> Forty years ago [in the 1970s], before we opened our shop here, earth and dust covered the entire area. People brought their carts there to sell vegetables or fruits. One day, a bulldozer came to remove some of the earth and

Figure 6.1. The grave ascribed to Sufiyan al-Thawri in Nablus in the form of a stone cuboid painted bright green. © Author

rocks scattered around there. When it hit the grave, it broke immediately. At this stage, people realized the presence of a pious man's grave at this location. They were uncertain as to who the person in the grave might be, but soon started referring to him as Sufiyan. It was evident that a person with strong faith lay buried there, someone loved by God who prayed a lot in his life.

The shopkeepers went on to explain how to know whether a pious person is buried somewhere: "In fact, the corpses of people who are very close to God remain the same after death. They do not decay or disintegrate [*dhāb*] in the way our bodies do. The dead person who is in the proximity of God experiences the time period between his death and the last day as merely five minutes of relaxing slumber." A middle-aged architect in Nablus agreed with this damaged-bulldozer version of the story and told me that the Nablus municipality had decided to assign the grave to Sufiyan al-Thawri and then named the adjacent street after him.

In yet another version, two men in their twenties stated that the name of "the person in this grave is unknown" and situated the story during the First Intifada of the late 1980s and early 1990s: "The only thing that is sure is that the man buried here is a pious man according to Islam [*ṣāliḥ al-islām*], a man who did no bad deed, but very many good deeds. People venerated this place for a long time. In the First Intifada, an Israeli tank hit it and immediately stopped functioning." All three versions describe incidents in which a human being, a bulldozer, or a tank is prevented from disturbing the grave, but they place the incidents at different historical moments. Another common element is that the storytellers agree that living a pious life intensifies the material and spiritual sustenance provided by God to the body of the deceased awaiting Judgment Day. While sinful persons are assumed to start tasting the tortures of hell right after their death, the pious man dwelling in his grave is said to enjoy certain comforts and perhaps even a glimpse of the pleasures of paradise. Consequently, all these versions of the story suggest that embodying virtue during one's lifetime influences the relative experience of time after death and protects the bodies of the pious from decaying and experiencing pain. In the case of this shrine, such postmortem materiality is able to paralyze or even kill foreign invaders and the technological equipment or scientific knowledge they use in their attempts to dislodge it.

The stories convey a firm conviction that embodying Islamic virtues in this life connects people with God, who can then provide them with His sustenance beyond death. These different versions of the myth turn the shrine into symbolic proof of a divine system of accounting and reward that is ultimately just. The meanings ascribed to the shrine validate this divine system of accounting and provision. Many of my interlocutors recognized that their livelihoods, even very modest ones, were an expression of divine sustenance and generosity. The conviction conveyed in such stories that God ultimately holds people accountable for injustice is meant to encourage Nablus inhabitants enduring the hardships of occupation to pursue an ideal of piety and virtuousness and laterally discipline others to do the same.

The Story of the Usurious Moneylender

Storytelling can also serve a disciplinary function by discouraging people from violating Islamic principles.[5] This is the case in stories that deprecate usury or charging interest on loans, which is explicitly forbidden in the Quran. Abd al-Rahim al-Hanbali, one of the members of the Nablus Zakat Committee (before the security crackdown) and the father of the martyr whose funeral was described above, told me the following story describing the divine negative consequences of moneylending:

> Practices of charging interest on loans [*ribā*] only reached Nablus in the 1920s with the arrival of the British. It is in this context of colonization that usury arose as an issue. At the time, a number of traders started to work with

foreigners who drew them into the practice of forbidden moneylending. As a result, God hit the families of these traders [with misfortune]. There is the case of one particular family whose name needs to remain secret. This family used to own a lot of land in the area, but due to their illicit speculations and practices of usurious lending, they became economically dead [*muḥikū*] and their family stopped having male descendants. Only a few of them stayed alive. Other traders engaged in usury were able to gauge the consequences of their actions in time and swiftly returned to the traditional practices of moneylending. Since the arrival of the British, various banks in Nablus practicing usurious lending went out of business. Currently, new usurious banks operate under the supervision of the Palestinian Authority. At some stage, they will also collapse.

This story has a disciplinary effect by suggesting that God has recently withdrawn His sustenance from businesses and even from entire lines of descent when men engaged in usurious moneylending. Not only does this discourage people from conducting such financial dealings but it also suggests that no one should do business with institutions involved in usurious moneylending, including banks operating under the oversight of the Palestinian Authority. In other words, the story encourages people to laterally discipline financial institutions by refraining from doing business with them, which could then put them out of business.

Historically, arrangements between influential families and foreign rulers (Ottoman, British, or Israeli) were crucial for economic success in Palestine, but talking openly about these matters can be very risky today. The fact that Hanbali refuses to disclose the name of the family that apparently stopped having male progeny points to the sensitivity of speaking about economic power in the context of foreign occupation. Political criticism tends to be voiced implicitly in the forms of rumors and stories such as this one.[6] Despite a certain vagueness, such stories have a disciplinary effect, if only to encourage people to live pious lives. Both the story of the shrine and the story of the usurious moneylenders seek to foster the disciplinary power of Islamic public culture in Nablus, as they contain implicit threats against those engaged in malpractice. In this sense, such moral storytelling functions as a form of lateral disciplining based on Islamic concepts reminding people that God holds them ultimately accountable even in an otherwise opaque and repressive political landscape.

The Limits of Lateral Disciplining in Economic Power Relations

Lateral disciplining based on storytelling, stickers and posters, and other forms of Islamic public culture has limits, however. This is illustrated by the fact that there are very wealthy people living in Nablus whose giving is framed as philanthropy rather than as a result of the social pressure to extract a rightful share. One of the wealthiest is Munib al-Masri, who in 2013 lived in a palace filled with expensive antiques from Europe; built on the edge of the southern mountain, the palace was visible from almost everywhere in Nablus. Having made a fortune in the Arab Gulf in various business sectors, including banking and the oil industry (Hanieh 2011, 93), Masri is a paradigmatic representative of the Palestinian transnational capitalist class. The Masri family constituted an important part of the conglomerates in the Arab Gulf that invest in the Palestinian territories through holding companies, including the Palestine Development and Investment Company (PADICO), which was established in 1993 and led by Masri (Hanieh 2011, 95). Masri allegedly benefited from his proximity to the Palestinian Authority and clearly belonged to the winners of the political economy of occupation while also being in an excellent position to scale up his investments if Palestinian statehood were to be achieved.

Masri's life trajectory tells the story of Palestinian class formation in the shadow of the Israeli expansions of 1948 and 1967, which displaced Palestinian capital to the Arab Gulf. The Arab Gulf's increasing economic domination and the internationalization of capital flows in the Middle East led to a hierarchical structure of Palestinian economic ownership, forming a "transnational class" (Hanieh 2011, 85). With the creation of the Palestinian Authority in 1994, Gulf capital held in part by Palestinian families started to flow back into the Palestinian economy. Indeed, the Oslo agreements opened up investment possibilities for transnational Palestinian elites. The architecture of these investment flows operate on three levels: conglomerates in the Gulf, holding companies in Palestine (linked to the Palestinian Authority), and companies and industrial zones that are established between Israeli and Palestinian territories (Hanieh 2011).[7] Therefore, the state building program of the Palestinian Authority under Israeli military rule is thought to primarily serve the economic interests of a wealthy segment of Palestinian society (Khalidi and Samour 2014, 187). This capitalist class, of which Masri is a prominent representative (fig. 6.2), arguably advanced its agenda by investing in sectors of the economy—such as service, banking, and information technology—that would allow its members to benefit within the politically tense context of the extensive security collaboration between Israel and the Palestinian Authority (Khalidi and Samour 2014, 193).[8]

When I discussed Masri's role in the city with people in the streets, they pointed out that his promises to create jobs via his investments had not materialized because he mainly invested in profitable enterprises like

Figure 6.2. Munib al-Masri wearing a uniform of the Palestinian National Security Service posing for a Western photographer in front of his palace above Nablus. © Jonas Opperskalski

telecommunications services sold to Palestinians in the occupied territories rather than in building up an export industry. A few people even went so far as to accuse Masri of being a miser who was always "serving tea to visitors rather than coffee, because it is cheaper." Attempts at laterally disciplining Masri through such gossip remained limited by the scale of his economic activities and wealth.

I personally met with Masri several times, taking a European journalist and a press photographer to visit his villa. Masri appeared to enjoy being portrayed in the Western press. On these occasions, he and I found out that we had both been living in Zurich, Switzerland, at the same time when he was running the branch office of the Arab Bank there. During one of our encounters, I asked him whether he paid zakat on his enormous wealth. Masri answered that he had already paid zakat on all his wealth as he accumulated it. His reply suggested that he considered zakat to be a kind of income tax rather than a wealth tax (i.e., the annual obligation to distribute or pay 2.5% on the wealth one is holding). Viewing zakat as a tax on income is an unorthodox interpretation that aligns with modern tax regimes, most of which largely focus on taxing income rather than total wealth. When I mentioned this interchange to Islamic sheikhs from the Jordanian Ministry of Awqaf and Religious Affairs during a visit to Amman, they admired my courage in asking Masri such a question but thought that Masri misunderstood the obligation to give zakat. If he had calculated zakat correctly, they assumed he might have had to extract a much more considerable amount of his wealth annually than what he was actually giving to charity. On the other hand, calculating what one owes in terms of zakat is obviously highly complex in the situation of a person such as Munib al-Masri. Many people in Nablus were convinced that many wealthy Arabs failed to pay their rightful share in zakat to the local Muslim community. Against this background, the social pressure arising from the Islamic public culture in the region (including the moral storytelling discussed above) had a limited effect on economic power relations and on disciplining the ultrawealthy into annually extracting at least 2.5 percent of their mobile wealth and spending it on the community.

While Hanbali was telling stories about families involved in capitalist practices being punished by God, the investor and philanthropist Masri seemed little affected by the moral risks arising from possibly not paying enough zakat. On the other hand, he played the role of what in contemporary North America and Europe is understood as a philanthropist. For example, he funded several socially beneficial construction projects in Nablus, including the restoration of parts of the old city and the expansion of the university, to which he donated a large building carrying his name. He also built a new mosque near his palace. Discussing the rise of the capitalist economic order in the United States and in Germany, Weber (1946, 308) argues that membership in Protestant sects enabled businesspeople to gain access to credit and important political and economic networks. While the extremely wealthy were often obliged to maintain certain kinds of ties to these sects, he observed that they remained surprisingly unaffected by the moral puritanism of these groups. I had a similar sense as I strolled through the streets of Nablus next to Masri while a European photographer snapped pictures of him. The Islamic public culture in Nablus, which echoes the moral puritanism of Protestant sects, and the social pressures it puts on people hardly seemed to affect Masri in his social and political role. For example, I was told that Hanbali and Masri sat on the same local committees tasked with developing the city and supporting its inhabitants. I suspect that their relationship to each other requires accepting that certain dilemmas remain unresolved. In this, they may be like less wealthy inhabitants of Nablus in having to navigate the ethical contradictions that arise from the everyday struggle to make a living under foreign military occupation while retaining a commitment to Islamic principles and virtues.

Ethical Problems in a Political Economy of Occupation

Almost all Palestinian initiatives intended to promote sustainable economic development in the occupied territories have been constrained by politics. Since the beginning of the occupation in 1967, Israel's economic policies have sought to curtail Palestinian development while establishing mechanisms of political control. The result is that Palestinian businesses in the West Bank and Gaza Strip have become increasingly dependent on the Israeli military administration that controls the economy (Roy 1995, 2007; Samara 2000).[9] In 1994, the Paris Protocol on Economic Relations signed by Israel and the Palestinian Liberation Organization as part of the ongoing peace process led to the establishment of a customs union between Israel and the newly created Palestinian Authority. Critics preferred a free trade agreement, rather than a customs union, as this would have given more sovereignty to the Palestinian Authority. The establishment of the customs union had severe consequences for Palestinian businesses as they could often only import goods from abroad through an Israeli partner firm. Moreover, the right to collect taxes and custom fees on behalf of the Palestinian Authority provided Israeli authorities with effective political leverage. Israel could withhold such revenues, which constituted up to 70 percent of the Palestinian Authority's budget (Taghdisi-Rad 2014, 23), and thereby exert political pressure at any moment.

Widespread suspicions about the injustice of the political system make the idea of divine bookkeeping (complemented by divine provision) attractive because it serves as a horizon for reflecting on and wrestling with ethical dilemmas arising from the ambition to live a good live under adverse circumstances.[10] In the eyes of my interlocutors, divine bookkeeping remains inaccessible to human perception and God's material sustenance can sometimes be delayed so it only reaches people after death. By giving the Other World a presence in their everyday lives in this world, people in Nablus are able to hold on to the idea that God's system of bookkeeping as a way of rewarding good deeds and sustaining the virtuous is ultimately just. In this logic, an insufficient income or means of making a living is not a sign that one is doing something wrong. While this stance invites a lot of guesswork, it ensures the plausibility of ultimate divine justice in the midst of a political economy of military occupation. The openness of the Islamic system as imagined by my interlocutors thus allows them to live with the contradictions and tensions that arise in their everyday lives.

The first dilemma arises out of the difficulty of remaining in Nablus and making a living without submitting to the occupying power—Israel—which is perceived as having unjustly taken over Palestinian land by force. Palestinian Muslims are encouraged to live a pious life and rely on God to sustain them materially, but their economic survival and ability to make a profit depend on submitting themselves to the economic power of the Israeli occupation. In other words, seeking a profit often requires some complicity with the injustice of the occupation. For example, textile workers depend on the owners of their workshops to obtain orders from Israeli businesspeople, and many other young construction workers are helping build Israeli settlements near Nablus. According to an imam of an old city mosque, taking such jobs is not reprehensible because people need to generate income to support their families. In a long conversation, a pious sewing worker told me that while his income was contingent on an Israeli businessman, he was still grateful for all the *rizq* that God was providing him in his life. Thus people look to divine justice to accommodate the contradictions of living under an occupying power.

Nablus residents found it more difficult to reconcile themselves to seeing members of the security forces continue to profit in opaque and unjust ways. They deplored the fact that the security forces controlled a considerable part of the economy, including foreign aid. The influx of foreign aid into the Palestinian territories since the Oslo agreements in 1994 became gradually aligned with Israel's exercise of political control over the Palestinian population. Aid from European and North American governments effectively privileged one kind of Palestinian elite over another while much of it was spent on training, financing, and, therefore, controlling Palestinian police and security forces (Turner 2014, 40). These security forces mainly protect the Palestinian Authority and Israel against insurgents from within the Palestinian territories, rather than the Palestinian population and its interests (43). Foreign donor practices since 1994 thus divided Palestinian society into winners and losers depending on individuals' degrees of acquiescence with Israeli security interests (46–47) and created conditions for the PA's increasing authoritarianism (El Kurd 2020).[11]

These wealth flows under a security regime reveal a contradiction. While aid is declared as supporting Palestinians, it is also perceived as molding Palestinian society into accepting continued Israeli settlement expansion. This contradiction exacerbated the dilemma of having to make a living in unjust circumstances. Neither piety nor hard work was seen to result in a steady income; rather, it was widely believed that one's proximity to aid flows and networks cultivated by non-Muslim foreign governments was necessary for survival. Under these conditions, the zakat committees before the security crackdown in 2007 gained an important symbolic character in the occupied Palestinian territories. They embodied an alternative to otherwise widespread corruption (Schaeublin 2009). Operating with funding from local and international sources beyond the control of the United States and European governments gained them a reputation for not being docile to these governments (Hilal and Maliki 1997, 62). In this context, they were seen as bypassing an established and largely corrupt architecture of economic domination.[12]

One way that Palestinian zakat committees before 2007 avoided charges of corruption was by aligning their handling of zakat funds with Islamic ethical principles. For example, a leaflet put out by the Ramallah Zakat Committee (1997, translation by the author) reminded its members as well as its donors about the extreme sensitivity of handling divine money: "Zakat funds are the right of their beneficiaries who are powerless and . . . [they] are unlike other funds. Whoever takes anything away from them in an illegal manner acts as if he took from the [hell] fire, and whoever takes from [these funds] in this life, this will be a woe [for him] in the Hereafter." This quote implies that divine bookkeeping entails high risks for anyone who does not treat zakat funds with the appropriate care. Presenting itself in such a way, the Ramallah Zakat Committee signaled to the public that its accountability was aligned with a divine system of justice. This enabled it to cultivate a reputation for integrity among Palestinians.

This again illustrates how the Other World shines through in this world to allow people to hold on to a sense of ultimate justice. Small gestures of mutual help as embodied in direct zakat transfers equally give a presence to the Other

World in the form of divine money embodying God's provision and power to sustain people. Giving zakat ties in with technologies of the self that allow people to pursue both a virtuous Muslim life in community with others and salvation in the Hereafter in spite of the adversity of the political conditions within which such lives unfold.

Divine bookkeeping also offers an alternative to the tensions that arise from living within a heavily surveilled society. Israeli intelligence has long since erected elaborate systems of surveillance and control by relying on collaboration with Palestinian secret services or Palestinian informants. Israeli military bureaucracy then accorded privilege to individuals depending on their wealth, job affiliation, and the security files kept in their names. Digital technologies continue to increase the scope of security surveillance in the occupied Palestinian territories and in the region more generally (Fatafta 2021). The full scope of how such new technologies, which are providing security agencies with an almost God-like (Fatafta 2021, 88; Tawil Souri 2017, 56) ability to track people's actions and conversations, will affect the Islamic public culture in places such as Nablus remains to be seen (for a discussion of surveillance technologies deployed around Islamic holy sites in Jerusalem, see Volinz 2018).

At the time of my fieldwork, the movements of the Palestinian population inside the West Bank and into Jordan or Israel (inside the 1967 borders) continued to be tied to a complex system of security clearances and permits (Kelly 2006). At border crossings and after political arrest operations, it was very common for Israeli security personnel to interrogate Palestinian travelers. On such occasions, the Israeli interrogators, who according to my Palestinian interlocutors could speak perfect Arabic, sometimes hinted that they knew minute details about people's personal lives.[13] It became clear to Nablus residents that Israeli authorities were able to keep an account of Palestinians' whereabouts and activities and would then resort to punishment or reward, for instance by either arresting people or providing them with security clearances. Under such circumstances, divine bookkeeping is particularly appealing because it suggests the existence of a parallel system that, relying on altogether different "principles of compensation and reward" (Weber 2004, 66) tied up with the Other World, continues to sustain human beings even as it eludes human understanding (Schaeublin 2021).

While the ethical dilemmas faced by Palestinians in the occupied territories may be particular to the region because they live under a non-Muslim ruling power, their experiences nevertheless resonate with questions regarding the social safety nets in other Arab countries in the Middle East whose populations also live under repressive governments.

Social Safety Nets in the Contemporary Middle East

One of the most prominent slogans of the Arab revolutions of 2011 was "Bread, freedom, dignity." Yet more than a decade after the governments of Egypt, Tunisia, and Yemen were toppled, the economic conditions in these countries remain dire. In Egypt, the counterrevolution led to a return to authoritarian rule. In Yemen, a complex intrastate war has still not come to an end. And in 2021, President Qais Saied suspended Tunisia's Parliament when protesters had again taken to the streets, disillusioned with Tunisia's political institutions because they failed to provide jobs or a minimum of social security.

Analyzing the American and the French Revolutions, Hannah Arendt (2018, 93) commented on the tension between the desire for freedom and the urgency of material need: "The men of the first revolutions, though they knew well enough that liberation had to precede freedom, were still unaware of the fact that such liberation means more than political liberation from absolute and despotic power; that to be free for freedom meant first of all to be free not only from fear but also from want." The Egyptian case, and perhaps also the Tunisian one, suggests that if material needs are not met, a return to authoritarian forms of governance can occur even though such forms of governance continue to fail to provide effective social safety nets. In the absence of functioning social safety nets and reliable employment, the citizens of many Arab countries rely on their families, tribal affiliations, and zakat donations to get by.

Two Tendencies in the Field of Zakat Distributions in the Middle East

Against this backdrop of renewed authoritarianism following the Arab revolutions, there appear to be two tendencies with a view to zakat collection and distribution in the Middle East. The first one is top down. Arab Gulf monarchies and wealthy zakat donors increasingly disburse zakat through humanitarian aid channels such as the United Nations High Commissioner for Refugees. In fact, the UN agency has been collecting fatwas from various Islamic institutions declaring it to be a legitimate vessel for zakat donations. At the same time, Islamic institutions operating in the humanitarian aid field continue to grow in importance (Petersen 2014); these are often funded by the Arab Gulf countries (Lacey and Benthall 2014). One question arising in this context is to what extent the quality of zakat as a social obligation and the connotations of justice that this entails (Mittermaier 2014) will continue to be a part of such distribution mechanisms, especially if they are controlled by authoritarian petro-monarchies in the Gulf (Derbal 2022).

The second tendency is bottom up. The ethnography of zakat in this book illustrates how people invoke Islamic texts to sustain systems of mutual help and direct giving. The zakat committee model described in chapter 2 is based on governments tolerating a certain degree of local self-organization to collect and distribute zakat. Such self-organization also occurred among Shi'i Muslim women in Southern Beirut (Deeb 2006) and Sunni Muslims in Egypt during the 2011 revolution (Mittermaier 2019). A strong sense of justice underlies Islamic acts of giving, which are framed as giving those in need their rightful share of God's provision. The question thus arises of how this socially distributed responsibility to look after others and give them their rightful share could be scaled up to contribute to building forms of statehood in Arab countries that will more effectively deliver services and provide social security.

In his conclusion to *The Gift*, Marcel Mauss ([1925] 2016) argues that industrialized, modern societies should take inspiration from nonmodern societies in making the heart of their social contract the obligation to give. Thus, the social contract spans rituals of giving between neighbors and relatives but also encompasses institutionalized forms of social insurance organized by syndicates or, indeed, the state. Mauss (192) even cites the Quran to describe an industrialized society in which giving is once again at the center of moral life and which he assumed, in 1925, to be "undergoing a laborious birth." If a new social contract based on a more just distribution of wealth is to emerge across Arab countries, the experiences of local zakat institutions and the mechanisms of reputation management and gossiping that hold them accountable could add constructive elements to such a process.[14]

Outlook

The practices of zakat in the political conditions of the contemporary Middle East deserve to be studied in comparative perspective with the ways in which wealth is ethically problematized in social interactions and political institutional landscapes in other regions of the world. In political and academic debates in Europe and North America, wealth is mainly discussed from the perspective of the state, which can impose more or less taxes and provide more or less comprehensive forms of social security. The "moral notion of gift... and of fortune" (Mauss [1925] 2016, 82) is rarely studied through ethnographies of face-to-face interactions and the ethical concepts that are invoked in them to reproduce or question power relations arising from differences of wealth (for a general discussion of which, see Graeber and Wengrow 2021). Studying the ethics of interaction in combination with political and social institutions could unearth a silent consensus (and the various ways of challenging it) that legitimizes and structures the flows of wealth through society. Such studies could not only open up comparative perspectives with social interactions in Muslim contexts, such as the one analyzed in this book, but also sharpen our understanding of the current state of the social contract in different political systems and the transformations of social safety nets in times of the rapid transformations of society induced by the spread of new digital technologies and the global push to reduce energy consumption.

NOTES

Introduction

1. For a detailed discussion of how to calculate the amount of zakat owed every year, see, for example, Singer (2008, 40–41).
2. For an overview of anthropological work on contemporary Palestine, see Atshan (2021).
3. An ethnography of interactions shaped by references to Islamic texts can be compared to other contexts where moral concepts are shaping face-to-face encounters (e.g., Keane 2015).
4. On the importance of Islamic concepts in greetings and everyday interactions, see Abu-Lughod (1989, 297), T. Asad and Scott (2006, 256, 234), and Moumtaz (2015, 128). For an ethnography on how Islamic concepts are invoked in interactions, see Rosen's (1984) *Bargaining for Reality*, which is rich in its discussion of the meanings of Arab terms, although limited when it comes to contextualizing the ethnographic material within history.
5. Hacking (2004) points out that Michel Foucault's and Erving Goffman's approaches to discourse complement each other. While Foucault tends to discuss discourse more "in the abstract," for instance, in how it shapes institutional orders, Goffman analyzes the presence of discourse in face-to-face interactions. Discursive categories can shape behavior and classify human beings at both levels, however.
6. According to Talal Asad (1993, 27–54; see also 1986), the focus on Islam as a religion is misleading because the term *religion*, as defined for example by Clifford Geertz ([1966] 1973) in his seminal essay "Religion as a Cultural System," inserts a problematic focus on belief. *Belief* has analytical connotations that are specific to European Christian history (Ruel 1992). Since the

Enlightenment, moreover, *religion* has come to describe one sphere of human activity in juxtaposition to other spheres such as politics, economics, or the law. In this sense, the term *religion* emerges from a specific classification of human activity that is neither universal nor historically stable.

7. In the anthropology of Islam, the shift to ethics has led to studies of how Muslims seek guidance on practical questions by consulting Islamic scholars (Agrama 2012; Messick 1993; Clarke 2010, 2018), coming together in groups to read and discuss Islamic texts (J. Bowen 1993, 7; Mahmood 2005), or listening to sermons on tapes and discussing their contents with fellow Muslims (Hirschkind 2006).

8. For a detailed discussion of the relation between interactions and acts of worship, see Hallaq (2014, 115–116, 203 fn. 69, 203–204 fn. 73).

9. Note that the tradition consistently considers orphans to be a subcategory of the poor (for a discussion of these two categories, see Benthall and Bellion-Jourdan 2009, 10). The Quran (76, 8) mentions that giving to children without a father (which results in their having only a fragile attachment to an agnatic kin group) is a sign of virtue.

10. See Qaradawi (2006) for a more recent development of this school of thought.

11. According to anthropologist Shirin Naef (pers. comm.), neither zakat nor the Shi'i concept for Islamic giving (*khums*) was included in Iran's tax system after the revolution of 1979. On *khums* and its relation to zakat, see Hayes (2017). For an account of how *khums* and zakat justify taxation in areas of Yemen held by Islamic armed "nonstate" actors, see Sana'a Center for Strategic Studies (2020).

12. For a discussion of how traditional discourses on zakat do not seek to challenge existing social structures and differences of class, consider the writings by the medieval Muslim scholar Al-Mawardi (d. 1058 AD) as discussed in Benthall and Bellion-Jourdan (2009, 15–16). In such traditional readings, we often encounter an inversion of hierarchy, whereby the wealthy are said to be dependent on the poor (Mittermaier 2019, 89). Consider Ghazali's ([1097] 1966, 42) description of the contemporaries of the Prophet who stretched out "their open palms so that the poverty-stricken man might take [sadaqa] therefrom and appear in the role of givers."

13. For a historical account of the tension between the leadership of PLO outside the occupied Palestinian territories and the Palestinian grassroots leadership within the territories under Israeli control, see Khatib (2010).

14. For a beautiful and well-researched historical novel discussing the manifold dimensions of life in Nablus in the early twentieth century, see Hammad (2019). Notice also that, since the 1990s, most of the Samaritans, while

maintaining friendly relations with the people of Nablus, have moved to a village on a nearby hill in the course of escalating violence between Israelis and Palestinians. As the sale of alcohol became impossible in Nablus during the Second Intifada, the Samaritans run liquor shops from their village in the mountains and supply the city with alcoholic beverages.

15. This book is neither another study of political Islam nor another analysis of Hamas's social role, even though this Palestinian Islamic movement remains prominent in Nablus. For literature on "political Islam" in Palestine, see Abu-Amr (1994), Milton-Edwards (1996), Baumgarten (2006), Hroub (2006), Tamimi (2007), and Roy (2011). For a theoretical analysis of the problems arising from inserting Islamic ethical thought into a state-oriented political project, see Hallaq (2014).
16. For detailed maps documenting continued Israeli settlement expansion around the city, see the website of the Israeli Human Rights organization Btselem: https://www.btselem.org. Against this background, a new generation of young men in Nablus resumed street fighting against Israeli military patrols in Nablus in 2022, using social media to publicize their actions.
17. This wording—which is also used by Israelis—is controversial as it marks separateness between Palestinians, which a Palestinian youth movement gaining steam since 2021 is trying to overcome.
18. For an analysis of the ethics of Palestinian nationalist commitment and the frustrations over the disintegration of the Palestinian nationalist movement during the Oslo period, see Allen (2013).
19. For an overview of the zakat sector in the Gaza Strip during the twentieth century, see Schaeublin (2012).
20. In general, *iṣlāḥ* committees are structures that practice *ṣulḥ*, the settlement of conflicts based on customary law with varying importance given to Islamic law. There are a variety of different *iṣlāḥ* committees in Palestine belonging to different political movements or big families. A number of zakat committees in the Gaza Strip simultaneously serve as *iṣlāḥ* committees. Other *iṣlāḥ* committees operate under the umbrella of the League of Scholars of Palestine.
21. On the interrogations of Palestinians, see, for example, Meari (2014). On political imprisonment, see Nashif (2008).

1. Fieldwork under Military Rule

1. On accusations of spying in the anthropology of the Middle East, see Dresch (2000) and Evans-Pritchard (1973, 9).
2. For a discussion of the role of influential families in Nablus in the context of soap factories, see the rich ethnography by Bontemps (2012).

3. Meneley (1996) provides an account of women's central role in upholding family status in visiting and hosting practices in Yemen, whereby the interior of the house can turn into a public space (on which, see also Vom Bruck 1997).
4. Some anthropologists have converted to Islam in the field, however. Emilio Spadola (2011), for instance, has written about the emotional, psychological, and relational tensions arising from his conversion during fieldwork in Morocco.
5. Personhood is not merely reflected or expressed through social interactions and greetings but rather created through them, as argued by Caton (1986, 291), drawing on ethnography from Yemen. Questions of autonomy and honor are central themes in the anthropological literature on personhood in the Middle East (see, e.g., Abu-Lughod [1986] 2016; Bourdieu 1965; Dresch 1989; Gilsenan 1976; Meneley 1996).
6. The tension between the obligation to discipline others and undue intrusion into others' affairs has given rise to a long-standing debate in the Islamic tradition (for an overview, see Cook 2001).
7. For a collection of such traditions, see, for example, the book of greetings in Nawawī ([1200s] 1975, 164–167). Many classical collections of Prophetic traditions contain a section specifically devoted to greetings.
8. On the social tensions arising from the use of *salām ʿalay-kum* (marking Islamic interaction) as opposed to simply saying good morning, see also Schielke's account from rural Egypt (2015, 5–6).
9. These two Ramadan greetings invoke God in the two roles discussed in the introduction: as (1) the Bookkeeper registering people's good and bad deeds and as (2) the ultimate and generous Provider of all sustenance.
10. Consider the scandals produced by early Orientalists in the nineteenth century who pointed out that the inhabitants of Mecca were smoking in private, as discussed by Dresch (2000).
11. For an outlook on an anthropology in conversation with an Islamic tradition, see Rasanayagam (2018).

2. Zakat Institutions on Shifting Grounds

1. This chapter is a revised version of an article previously published in the *Journal of Muslim Philanthropy & Civil Society*. See Schaeublin (2020).
2. For a rough overview of laws regulating Islamic charitable giving in Palestine since the late nineteenth century, see Challand (2009).
3. Based on historical anthropology of Lebanon, Moumtaz (2021) argues that modern statecraft has refigured the Islamic practice of charitable

endowment (*waqf*) by giving rise of a new architecture of state, law, and religion accompanying a new property regime under a secular legal arrangement.

4. Amin Maqbul, interview with the author, November 11, 2014. Maqbul was serving as president of the charitable society at the time.
5. On these origins, see also Schaeublin (2009, 16). The establishment of the NZC in the 1970s was encouraged by Abdul-'Aziz al-Khayyat, a Jordanian sheikh who has written a book on applying zakat in practice (Khayyat 1993). He apparently played a key role in providing the committee with official Jordanian support. See, e.g., Schaeublin (2009, 35). For an account of Khayyat's thoughts on zakat, see Benthall and Bellion-Jourdan (2009, 10–13, 16–17). See also Schaeublin (2009, 16). As declared guardian over the Islamic holy sites in Jerusalem, the state of Jordan governed Islamic affairs, including zakat, sadaqa, and *waqf* lands (*awqāf*) in different parts of Palestine through their representation office in Jerusalem. On the political role of Jordanians in governing Islamic institutions and discourse in this period, see Abu-Amr (1994, 14), Dumper (2002), and Milton-Edwards (1996).
6. See Schaeublin (2009, 30).
7. *Waqf*s significantly shaped the architecture of the city of Jerusalem; see, for instance, Sroor (2012).
8. Adly Yaish, interview with the author, October 28, 2013. For a genealogical perspective on such *waqf* practices in the region, see Moumtaz (2021).
9. Before the political turmoil in the zakat sector in 2008, this project had an exemplary reputation (Schaeublin 2009, 26).
10. Notice that the zakat committees in Jerusalem stayed under Jordanian jurisdiction (Iwais and Schaeublin 2011).
11. For details, see Schaeublin (2009, 17).
12. For details, see Schaeublin (2009, 49).
13. For an overview of the consequences of the closures, see Schaeublin (2009, 46–48).
14. See Schaeublin (2012, 79).
15. On the practice of hiding need in Nablus, see Schaeublin (2019).
16. The 1990 Management and Finance Regulations (Article 14b) of the Jordanian zakat law state that all donations must be registered with cash receipts.
17. Article 8a of the Jordanian zakat law lists the following categories for spending zakat: "The poor [*fuqarā'*] and the needy [*masākīn*]; poor students; orphans, the geriatric, the poor, the disabled, and the institutions that take care of them; the poor sick and the institutions that take care of them; foreigners in need; publication [of leaflets] that incite [people to adhere] to Islamic practice [*da'wa*] and the poor [persons] working in [the field of calling others to Islam]; those afflicted with misfortune without [their]

wrongdoing [ma'aṣiyya] because of a flood, a bankruptcy, a fire, an earthquake, or another [misfortune]; and necessary activities for managing the [zakat] fund, provided that expenditures do not annually exceed ten percent of the income of the fund."

18. The meanings of *jihad* have given rise to considerable discussion. For a discussion of the very different political projects that jihad can give rise to, see Li (2020). For a discussion by a contemporary Islamic scholar of "in the way of God" as a beneficiary category of zakat and its links to jihad, see Qaradawi (2006, 2:57–73). The nineteenth-century Islamic studies scholar Goldziher (1890, 390–391) argues that while this phrase was first interpreted in the context of warfare (*jihad*), it has gradually been extended to include every action that pleases God, such as giving sadaqa through the establishment of public fountains (themselves called *sabīl*, the word used for "way").

19. This question has also led to a difference of view among researchers, which I will not go into here. For more on this, see Levitt (2006); Benthall (2008, 2017); Schaeublin (2009, 2012).

20. World-Check has in the meantime been bought up by Thomson Reuters (Schaeublin 2012, 64–65; see also James 2019b, 156–157). In 2018, Blackstone bought a majority stake of the Thomson Reuters Financial Risk Unit, of which World-Check was a part. As a result of the deal, the unit was renamed Refinitiv (Reuters 2018).

21. PA Ministry of Awqaf, interview with the author, June 12, 2019.

22. Soup kitchens play an important role in contemporary Cairo (Mittermaier 2019) and Jerusalem under Ottoman rule (Singer 2012). The 550-year-old Takkiyah Khāṣqī Sulṭān soup kitchen is now run by the Jerusalem Zakat Committee (Iwais and Schaeublin 2011, 164). Another famous soup kitchen in the West Bank belongs to the mosque in Hebron containing the tomb of Prophet Abraham, known for his exemplary pious generosity (Stillman 2017, 217 n26).

3. Concealing and Exposing Need

1. This statement is from an Aljazeera documentary about the Hammouz Café, which is part of a series called *Maqāhī 'Atīqa* [Old-fashioned cafés] available online. Accessed January 1, 2019. https://www.youtube.com/watch?v=Oo8zlUz54Jg.

2. Only 8.9 percent of the workforce of the Nablus governorate worked in Israel or Israeli settlements, a number considerably lower than in all other West Bank governorates (PCBS 2015, 20). For details, see the Palestinian Central Bureau of Statistics (PCBS 2015, 19). Note that the Gaza

governorates had considerably lower average wages and significantly higher rates of unemployment in the same period (19).
3. The focus of this chapter is on direct zakat giving between families and individual people. There are, however, other informal zakat practices. In Palestine, not all zakat committees were formally registered (Schaeublin 2009). At the time of my fieldwork, such informal committees were illegal. For this reason, I have not undertaken inquiries into the existence of such structures.
4. For a discussion of the word *'ayb* in tribal Yemen, see Dresch (1989, 39–41), who renders it as "disgrace" or "insult" used to judge any public incident that breaks or damages honor (*sharaf*).
5. Notice that the ambiguity of the English term *to cover* is also retained in the Arabic word *satara*.
6. For a critique of this argument, see Ismail (2007).
7. See Perdigon (2015, 94) for a parallel observation from Lebanon.
8. The derivative *istiḥyā'* (used as a verb by the woman above and Qusay later in this chapter) highlights this active element of shame more explicitly. It is translated as "making oneself look shy or ashamed in front of others." In Palestine, the verb derived from *istiḥyā'* is also used to tell guests not to refrain from eating and drinking. People say, "Don't be shy" (*btistaḥīsh*).
9. According to Meneley (1996, 82), the obligation to actively display shyness is partly about channeling and controlling female sexuality. Like material need, female sexual desire requires particular efforts at covering or concealment, as its visibility can directly affect the honor of male relatives. In conservative contexts, women displaying shyness prove that they are aware of the appropriate behavior expected from them. Like poor people's concealment of their need, female modesty appears to constitute Meneley's women interlocutors as moral persons. In Meneley's (1996) account, deference and status play an important role. In her fieldwork, she encountered clearly defined status groups. In Nablus, I did not find such clearly defined categories of status.
10. With a view to sexual needs, *ḥayā'* refers to chastity (cf. Mahmood 2005, 23, 100–104, 155–161).
11. For a discussion of such workshops, see Natsheh and Parizot (2016). Since the 1990s, free trade and special industrial zones have been established in Jordan, Egypt, and the Gulf. These facilities promoted "minimum worker rights, low wages and taxes, and full profit repatriation in order to entice foreign investors [including Israeli] to set up shop" (Hanieh 2011, 88; see also Hanieh 2013). This process diminished the textile production in the West Bank. The workshop in Nablus that I am describing here was, in a

certain way, a remnant of what once was a much wider landscape of textile production.
12. For a literary account of such "pressures" in a different Arabic-speaking and Islamic context, see the short story by Tayeb Salih ([1953] 1970) "A Date Palm by the Stream." The story is set in a village on the Sudanese Nile, where a merchant bullies an old man with a lot of debt to sell a beautiful palm tree that the old man planted in his youth. The old man's trust in God (*tawakkul*) and self-respect is put to the test.
13. For a sharp literary account of the tensions surrounding such anonymous "deals" between affluent and destitute persons, see the play *Dans la Solitude des Champs de Coton* by Bernard-Marie Koltès (1986).
14. For a detailed discussion of this dilemma, see Schaeublin (2019).
15. Historically, the social perception of poor people in the Islamic tradition oscillates between admiration of their pious self-restraint (*ta'affuf*) and skepticism regarding the veracity of their financial need. This ambiguity in the perception of poverty reaches back into the premodern Islamic tradition (Herzog 2011).

4. The Piety of Giving

1. Besides the issue of shame discussed in the previous chapter, recipients of aid were also hesitant to speak openly about the support they receive out of fear that this might prevent them from accessing aid from other sources in the future.
2. See also the Quran (2, 262–263): "They who spend their possessions for the sake of God and do not thereafter mar their spending by stressing their own benevolence and hurting [the feelings of the needy] shall have their reward with their Sustainer, and no fear need they have, and neither shall they grieve. A kind word and the veiling of another's want is better than a charitable deed followed by hurt; and God is self-sufficient, forbearing."
3. Even zakat institutions considered such knowledge distributed among networks in the neighborhoods reliable, and they would send social workers to ask around if they wanted to triangulate their needs assessment of a family on their beneficiary lists.
4. For a discussion of the limits of depersonalizing gifts, see Laidlaw (2000).
5. Ethnography from the Turkish town of Kayseri suggests that zakat practice can have a transformative effect on the giver, for example, by removing "racialized and discriminatory dispositions" in the perception of Kurds and Roma (Alkan-Zeybek 2012, 148–149). In this context, a wealthy woman is cited who overcomes her revulsion when visiting poor households and who

interprets her newfound ability to eat and socialize with lower-class people as a positive change of her ethical disposition.
6. For a similar ethnographic example from Morocco, see D. Bowen (2002, 264–265).
7. For an extensive discussion of "divine bookkeeping" as a "technology of the self" in historical perspective, see Schaeublin (2021).
8. On the other hand, I was often told that nobody enters paradise merely because of his or her deeds (or points) and that this is solely contingent on God's mercy. In the first centuries of the Islamic tradition, this issue was debated by different schools of scriptural interpretation. While the Kharijites held that certain sinful acts could render a person non-Muslim, the Murjites argued that faith in and submission to God superseded acts of piety and good deeds (see, e.g., Fakhry 2004, 40–41). This seems largely to be in analogy with the debates around faith and work in Christian theology, suggesting that there are important commonalities between the Christian and Islamic traditions surrounding the issues of merit and giving.
9. For examples from a South Asian context, see Cort (2003).
10. See also chapter 5. For a discussion of the history and architecture of these fountains in Nablus, see Qaddumi (2012) and Arafat (2013).
11. According to my interlocutors, only 30 percent of the mosques in Nablus were staffed with an imam employed by the Palestinian Authority. In the remaining mosques, volunteers led the prayers, yet almost all mosques were operating at full capacity and many were overflowing during Friday prayer. Another reason for the mosques' inability to cover people's needs is that any suggestion of Islamic political activism in mosques faced harsh repression. Some sheikhs in Nablus had adopted a more aggressive stance by defending armed resistance against Israeli occupation as a viable option for improving people's living conditions and by arguing that mosques should serve as a space of political mobilization against injustice. At the same time, Palestinian security apparatuses collaborating intensely with the Israeli authorities closely monitored anything that went on inside mosques.

5. The Ethics of Giving and Market Transactions

1. In other ethnographic examples, such as from South Asia, the gift can be poisonous because the object given is believed to contain the personal substance of the giver (Mauss [1925] 2016).
2. This development is largely the result of rich locals and Palestinians living abroad investing in real estate.
3. Most people do not dare to walk into the inner parts of the old city at night. After midnight, Israeli armed forces run regular operations in the old city

to arrest people. Sometimes they face armed resistance while doing so, albeit nowhere close to the intensity of the street fighting during the Second Intifada. The likelihood of such interventions turns the old city alleys at night into an almost lawless space giving rise to myths and rumors about illicit, immoral, and even supernatural encounters that are said to take place there.
4. The idea of *rizq* does not imply fatalism. It is rather connected to an understanding of human existence as "a space of potentialities set out by God, which men must serendipitously navigate and explore without completely mastering" (Gaibazzi 2015, 227). In exploring these potentialities, humans are called to rely on God. For an ethnographic exploration of how the notion of *rizq* affects real estate speculation in contemporary Lahore, see Rahman (2022).
5. In the sense of what Foucault (1997, 225) defines as "technologies of the self" (see the introduction).
6. In the first centuries of the Islamic tradition, this issue was debated by different schools of scriptural interpretation. While the Kharijites held that certain sinful acts could render a person non-Muslim, the Murjites argued that faith in and submission to God superseded acts of piety and good deeds (see, e.g., Fakhry 2004, 40–41).
7. After the Reformation, however, several Protestant sects appeared to combine an ideal of Christian piety with the pursuit of financial success in trade (Weber [1905] 2012). Consider also the Quakers, for instance.
8. For a discussion of the importance of gestures and expressions in sale contracts in the Islamic discursive tradition, see, for example, Messick (2001) on sharia scholars in Yemen.

6. The Other World and the Occupation

1. For discussions of steadfastness (*ṣumūd*) in the Palestinian context more generally, see, for example, Meari (2014) and Ryan (2015). Note also the Islamic connotation of the term. The Quran (112, 2) describes God as *al-ṣamad* (from the same root as *ṣumūd*), the one who persists and the Sustainer of all.
2. Note that Palestinians under Israeli occupation live very different lives, many of which do not align with the Islamic ideas and framings that emerge from my ethnography of public culture in Nablus.
3. For an extensive discussion linking Islamic shrines to contemporary issues and politics, see Sevea (2020).
4. For his historical role, see, for example, Cook (2001, 65–67, 92, 99–102).
5. For a discussion of the moral or ethical power of historical narratives such as these, see White (1980).

6. On the sensitivity of recounting the history of families in Jordan, see Shryock (1995, 1997).
7. On the Palestinian political economy, see also Leech (2016).
8. Among Palestinians, the project of combining nationalist institution building under Israeli occupation with a policy of attracting deregulated transnational investments is highly contested. According to Hanieh (2011, 99), the opposition to these policies coalesced around different Islamic movements, of which Hamas was the most prominent: "They have often directed their rhetoric towards the poorest and most marginalized layers of Palestinian society in the West Bank and Gaza Strip. Hamas does not possess the same close linkages with the Palestinian capitalist class shown by Fatah and the mainstream wings of the PLO. At the same time, these class differences require nuanced interpretation. Hamas has historically drawn much of its material support from fundraising efforts in the Gulf region, and its religious character has made it difficult for the movement to distance itself from Gulf regimes such as Saudi Arabia."
9. For a literary account of how the process of becoming economically dependent on Israel affected personal relations in Nablus during the 1970s, see Khalifeh ([1976] 1999).
10. In the volatile and capitalist political economies, the idea of invisible or "occult" parallel systems of value seems to be particularly attractive. In postapartheid South Africa, for instance, "occult economies" connected to witchcraft practices were thriving (Comaroff and Comaroff 1999).
11. International donors, such as Western development agencies and international NGOs, exercised a "power to promote and to exclude" (Challand 2009) over local NGOs as a form of politically disciplining civil society.
12. In other contexts, where Muslims exercise repressive power and dominate the politics of aid flows, institutions distributing zakat may have an altogether different reputation and role.
13. For an ethnographic take on the encounter of Israelis interrogating Palestinians, see, for example, Meari (2014). For an extensive account of the political imprisonment of Palestinians in Israel, see Nashif (2008).
14. For a discussion of similar reputation-based trust and accountability mechanisms on the level of business relations in a politically unstable context, see Choudhury's (2022, 342) study of the regulation of trade credit by money exchangers in contemporary Afghanistan operating on the level of "mundane, day-to-day transactions."

REFERENCES

Abu-Amr, Ziad. 1994. *Islamic Fundamentalism in the West Bank and Gaza.* Bloomington: Indiana University Press.
Abu-Lughod, Lila. (1986) 2016. *Veiled Sentiments: Honor and Poetry in a Bedouin Society.* Berkeley: University of California Press.
———. 1989. "Zones of Theory in the Anthropology of the Arab World." *Annual Review of Anthropology* 18 (1): 267–306.
Agrama, Hussein. 2012. *Questioning Secularism: Islam, Sovereignty, and the Rule of Law in Modern Egypt.* Chicago: University of Chicago Press.
Alkan-Zeybek, Hilal. 2012. "Ethics of Care, Politics of Solidarity: Islamic Charitable Organisations in Turkey." In *Ethnographies of Islam: Ritual Performances and Everyday Practices*, edited by Baudouin Dupret, Thomas Pierret, Paulo G. Pinto, and Kathryn Spellman-Poots, 144–152. Edinburgh: Edinburgh University Press.
Allen, Lori. 2013. *The Rise and Fall of Human Rights: Cynicism and Politics in Occupied Palestine.* Stanford, CA: Stanford University Press.
Anderson, Paul. 2011. "'The Piety of the Gift': Selfhood and Sociality in the Egyptian Mosque Movement." *Anthropological Theory* 11 (3): 3–21.
Arafat, Naseer Rahmi. 2013. *Nablus: City of Civilizations.* Nablus: CHEC.
Arendt, Hannah. 2018. *The Freedom to be Free.* New York: Penguin Classics.
Asad, Muhammad. 1980. *The Message of the Qur'ān.* Gibraltar: Dar al-Andalus.
Asad, Talal. 1973. *Anthropology and the Colonial Encounter.* London: Ithaca.
———. 1986. "The Idea of an Anthropology of Islam." Occasional Paper Series, Centre for Contemporary Arab Studies, Georgetown University, Washington, DC.
———. 1993. *Genealogies of Religion: Discipline and Reasons of Power in Christianity and Islam.* Baltimore: Johns Hopkins University Press.

———. 2003. *Formations of the Secular: Christianity, Islam, Modernity.* Stanford, CA: Stanford University Press.

———. 2020. "Thinking about Religion through Wittgenstein." *Critical Times* 3 (3): 403–442.

Asad, Talal, and David Scott. 2006. "The Trouble of Thinking: An Interview with Talal Asad." In *Powers of the Secular Modern: Talal Asad and His Interlocutors,* edited by David Scott and Charles Hirschkind, 243–304. Stanford, CA: Stanford University Press.

Atia, Mona. 2013. *Building a House in Heaven: Pious Neoliberalism and Islamic Charity in Egypt.* Minneapolis: University of Minnesota Press.

Atshan, Sa'ed. 2021. "The Anthropological Rise of Palestine." *Journal of Palestine Studies* 50 (4): 3–31.

Bashear, Suliman. 1993. "On the Origins and Development of the Meaning of Zakāt in Early Islam." *Arabica* 40 (1): 84–113.

Baumgarten, Helga. 2006. *Hamas: Der politische Islam in Palästina.* Munich: Heinrich Hugendubel.

Benthall, Jonathan. 2008. "The Palestinian Zakat Committees 1993–2007 and Their Contested Interpretations." PSIO Occasional Paper 1/2008, Graduate Institute of International and Development Studies, Geneva. (Reprinted in Benthall 2016, 57–80.)

———. 2011a. "Islamic Humanitarianism in an Adversarial Context." In *Forces of Compassion: Humanitarianism between Ethics and Politics,* edited by Erica Bornstein and Peter Redfield, 95–121. Santa Fe: SAR Press.

———. 2011b. "An Unholy Tangle: Boim versus the Holy Land Foundation." *UCLA Journal of Islamic and Near Eastern Law* 10 (1): 1–10. (Reprinted in Benthall 2016, 99–107.)

———. 2016. *Islamic Charities and Islamic Humanism in Troubled Times.* Manchester: Manchester University Press.

———. 2017. "Experto Crede? A Legal and Political Conundrum." In *If Truth Be Told: The Politics of Public Ethnography,* edited by Didier Fassin, 160–186. Raleigh, NC: Duke University Press.

———. 2021. "Friend, Foe, or in Between? Humanitarian Action and the Soviet Afghan War." In *Rebel Economies: Warlords, Insurgents, Humanitarians,* edited by Nicola Di Cosimo, Didier Fassin, and Clémence Pinaud, 181–203. Lanham: Lexington Books.

Benthall, Jonathan, and Jérôme Bellion-Jourdan. 2009. *The Charitable Crescent: Politics of Aid in the Muslim World.* New York: I. B. Tauris.

Bhungalia, Lisa. 2015. "Managing Violence: Aid, Counterinsurgency, and the Humanitarian Present in Palestine." *Environment and Planning A: Economy and Space* 47 (11): 2308–2323.

Biersteker, Thomas, and Sue Eckert, eds. 2008. *Countering the Financing of Terrorism*. London: Routledge.

Bontemps, Véronique. 2012. *Ville et patrimoine en Palestine. Une ethnographie des savonneries de Naplouse*. Paris: IISMM Karthala.

Bourdieu, Pierre. 1965. "The Sentiment of Honour in Kabyle Society." In *Honour and Shame: The Values of Mediterranean Society*, edited by Jean Péristiany, 193–241. London: Weidenfeld and Nicolson.

Bowen, Donna Lee. 2002. "Abu Illya and Zakat." In *Everyday Life in the Muslim Middle East*, edited by Donna L. Bowen and Evelyn A. Early, 262–265. Bloomington: Indiana University Press.

Bowen, John Richard. 1993. *Muslims through Discourse: Religion and Ritual in Gayo Society*. Princeton, NJ: Princeton University Press.

Brown, Nathan J. 2003. *Palestinian Politics after the Oslo Accords: Resuming Arab Palestine*. Berkeley: University of California Press.

Bukhārī, Muḥammad ibn Ismāʿīl al-. 1979. *Ṣaḥīḥ al-Bukhārī: The Translation of the Meanings of Ṣaḥīḥ al-Bukhārī (Arabic and English)*. Translated by M. M. Khan. Chicago.

Cammett, Melani. 2014. *Compassionate Communalism: Welfare and Sectarianism in Lebanon*. Ithaca, NY: Cornell University Press.

Caton, Steven. 1986. "Salāam Taḥīyah: Greetings from the Highlands of Yemen." *American Ethnologist* 13 (2): 290–308.

Challand, Benoît. 2009. *Palestinian Civil Society: Foreign Donors and the Power to Promote and Exclude*. London: Routledge.

Choudhury, Nafay. 2022. "Transacting on Trust: The Regulation of Trade Credit by Afghanistan's Money Exchangers." *Transnational Law and Contemporary Problems* 31 (2): 342–372.

Clark, Janine. 2004. *Islam, Charity, and Activism: Middle-Class Networks and Social Welfare in Egypt, Jordan, and Yemen*. Bloomington: Indiana University Press.

Clarke, Morgan. 2010. "Neo-Calligraphy: Religious Authority and Media Technology in Contemporary Shiite Islam." *Comparative Studies in Society and History* 52 (2): 351–383.

———. 2013. "Integrity and Commitment in the Anthropology of Islam." In *Articulating Islam: Anthropological Approaches to Muslim Worlds*, edited by Magnus Marsden and Konstantinos Retsikas, 209–227. New York: Springer.

———. 2018. *Islam and Law in Lebanon: Sharia within and without the State*. Cambridge: Cambridge University Press.

Comaroff, Jean, and John Comaroff. 1999. "Occult Economies and the Violence of Abstraction: Notes from the South African Postcolony." *American Ethnologist* 26 (2): 279–303.

Cook, Michael. 2001. *Commanding Right and Forbidding Wrong in Islamic Thought*. Cambridge: Cambridge University Press.

Cort, John. 2003. "Doing for Others: Merit Transfer and Karma Mobility in Jainism." In *Jainism and Early Buddhism: Essays in Honor of Padmanabh S. Jaini*, edited by Olle Qvarnström, 129–150. Fremont, CA: Asian Humanities Press.

De Cordier, Bruno. 2010. "Facing the Challenges of Social Upliftment and Definition of Identity: A Field Analysis of the Jamaat-e-Islami Hind's Social Service Wing Network in Meerut, India." *Journal of Muslim Minority Affairs* 30 (4): 479–500.

Deeb, Lara. 2006. *An Enchanted Modern: Gender and Public Piety in Shi'i Lebanon*. Princeton, NJ: Princeton University Press.

de Goede, Marieke. 2012. *Speculative Security: The Politics of Pursuing Terrorist Monies*. Minneapolis: University of Minnesota Press.

Derbal, Nora. 2022. *Charity in Saudi Arabia: Civil Society under Authoritarianism*. Cambridge: Cambridge University Press.

Doughty, Charles. (1888) 1936. *Travels in Arabia Deserta*. London: Cape.

Doumani, Beshara. 1995. *Rediscovering Palestine: Merchants and Peasants in Jabal Nablus, 1700–1900*. Berkeley: University of California Press.

———. 1998. "Endowing Family: Waqf, Property Devolution, and Gender in Greater Syria, 1800 to 1860." *Comparative Studies in Society and History* 40 (1): 3–41.

Dresch, Paul. 1989. *Tribes, Government, and History in Yemen*. Oxford: Oxford University Press.

———. 1998. "Mutual Deception: Totality, Exchange, and Islam in the Middle East." In *Marcel Mauss: A Centenary Tribute*, edited by Wendy James and N. J. Allen, 111–133. Oxford: Berghahn.

———. 2000. "Wilderness of Mirrors: Truth and Vulnerability in Middle Eastern Fieldwork." In *Anthropologists in a Wider World: Essays on Field Research*, edited by Paul Dresch, Wendy James, and David Parkin, 109–128. Oxford: Berghahn.

Dumper, Michael. 2002. *The Politics of Sacred Space: The Old City of Jerusalem in the Middle East Conflict*. Boulder, CO: Lynne Rienner.

El Kurd, Dana. 2020. *Polarized and Demobilized: Legacies of Authoritarianism in Palestine*. Oxford: Oxford University Press.

Elyachar, Julia. 2005. *Markets of Dispossession: NGOs, Economic Development, and the State in Cairo*. Raleigh, NC: Duke University Press.

Erie, Matthew. 2016. "Sharia, Charity, and *Minjian* Autonomy in Muslim China: Gift Giving in a Plural World." *American Ethnologist* 43 (2): 311–324.

Evans-Pritchard, Edward E. 1973. "Some Reminiscences and Reflections on Fieldwork." *Journal of the Anthropological Society of Oxford* 4 (1): 1–12.

REFERENCES

Fakhry, Majid. 2004. *A History of Islamic Philosophy*. New York: Columbia University Press.
Falcioni, Daniela. 2012. "Conceptions et pratiques du don en Islam." *Revue du MAUSS* 39 (1): 443–464.
Fanon, Frantz. (1952) 2008. *Black Skin, White Masks*. Northampton: Pluto.
Fatafta, Marwa. 2021. "Algorithms of Occupation: The Use of Artificial Intelligence in Israel and Palestine." In *Human Rights Responsibilities in the Digital Age: States, Companies and Individuals*, edited by Jonathan Andrew and Frédéric Bernard, 75–92. Oxford: Hart.
Fauzia, Amelia. 2013. *Faith and the State: A History of Islamic Philanthropy in Indonesia*. Leiden: Brill.
Foucault, Michel. 1986. *The Care of the Self: The History of Sexuality*. Vol. 3. New York: Pantheon.
———. 1997. "Technologies of the Self." In *Ethics: Subjectivity, Truth—Essential Works of Foucault, 1954–1984*, edited by Paul Rabinow, 223–251. New York: New Press.
Gaibazzi, Paolo. 2015. "The Quest for Luck: Fate, Fortune, Work and the Unexpected among Gambian Soninke Hustlers." *Critical African Studies* 7 (3): 227–242.
Geertz, Clifford. (1966) 1973. "Religion as a Cultural System." In *The Interpretation of Cultures*. New York: Basic Books.
———. (1968) 2004. *Islam Observed*. New Haven, CT: Yale University Press.
Ghazali, Abu Hamid al-. (1097) 1966. *The Mysteries of Almsgiving: A Translation from the Arabic with Notes of the Kitāb Asrār al-Zakāh of al-Ghazālī's Iḥiyā' 'Ulūm al-Dīn*. Translated by Nabih Amin Faris. Beirut: Centennial Publications, American University of Beirut.
Gilsenan, Michael. 1976. "Lying, Honor, and Contradiction." In *Transaction and Meaning: Directions in the Anthropology of Exchange and Symbolic Behavior*, edited by Bruce Kapferer, 191–219. Philadelphia: Institute for the Study of Human Issues.
———. 1996. *Lords of the Lebanese Marches: Violence and Narrative in an Arab Society*. Berkeley: University of California Press.
Goffman, Erving. 1959. *The Presentation of the Self in Everyday Life*. London: Allen Lane.
Goldziher, Ignaz. 1890. *Muhammedanische Studien: Theil Zwei*. Halle: Niemeyer.
Graeber, David. 2011. *Debt: The First 5000 Years*. New York: Melville House.
Graeber, David, and David Wengrow. 2021. *The Dawn of Everything: A New History of Humanity*. New York: Farrar, Straus and Giroux.
Haaretz. 2003. "Naval Commando Killed in Nablus." September 7, 2003. https://www.haaretz.com/2003-09-07/ty-article/naval-commando-killed-in-nablus/0000017f-dec0-db22-a17f-fef18cbf0000.

Hacking, Ian. 2004. "Between Michel Foucault and Erving Goffman: Between Discourse in the Abstract and Face-to-Face Interaction." *Economy and Society* 33 (3): 277–302.

Hallaq, Wael. 2009. *Sharia: Theory, Practice, Transformations*. Cambridge: Cambridge University Press.

———. 2014. *The Impossible State: Islam, Politics, and Modernity's Moral Predicament*. New York: Columbia University Press.

Hammad, Isabella. 2019. *The Parisian*. New York: Grove.

Hanieh, Adam. 2011. "The Internationalisation of Gulf Capital and Palestinian Class Formation." *Capital & Class* 35:81–106.

———. 2013. *Lineages of Revolt: Issues of Contemporary Capitalism in the Middle East*. Chicago: Haymarket Books.

Hayes, Edmund. 2017. "Alms and the Man: Fiscal Sectarianism in the Legal Statements of the Shiʿi Imams." *Islamic Law* 17:280–298.

Hegghammer, Thomas. 2010. *Jihad in Saudi Arabia*. Cambridge: Cambridge University Press.

Henig, David. 2019. "Economic Theologies of Abundance: Halal Exchange and the Limits of Neoliberal Effects in Post-war Bosnia-Herzegovina." *Ethnos* 84 (2): 223–240.

Herzog, Thomas. 2011. "Figuren der Bettler." *Asiatische Studien* 65 (1): 67–94.

Hilal, Jamil, and Majdi Maliki. 1997. *Muʾassasāt li-l-Daʿm al-Ijtimāʿī fī al-Ḍaffa al-Gharbiyya wa al-Qiṭāʿ Ghazza* [Social support institutions in the West Bank and the Gaza Strip]. Ramallah: Palestine Economic Policy Research Institute, MAS.

Hirschkind, Charles. 2006. *The Ethical Soundscape: Cassette Sermons and Islamic Counterpublics*. New York: Columbia University Press.

Hroub, Khaled. 2006. "A 'New Hamas' through Its New Documents." *Journal of Palestine Studies* 35 (4): 6–27.

Hurgronje, Snouck. (1882) 1957. "La zakat." In *Snouck Hurgronje: Oeuvres choisies*, edited by Georges-Henri Bousquet and Joseph Schacht, 150–170. Leiden: Brill.

Ibn Hazm, Ali Ibn Ahmad. (1022) 1953. *The Ring of the Dove*. Translated by Arthur J. Arberry. London: Luzac Oriental.

International Crisis Group. 2008. *Ruling Palestine II: The West Bank Model?* July 17, 2008. https://www.crisisgroup.org/middle-east-north-africa/eastern-mediterranean/israelpalestine/ruling-palestine-ii-west-bank-model.

Ishtiyya, Mohammed. 2008. *Mawsūʿa al-Muṣṭalaḥāt w-al-Mafāhīm al-Filasṭīniyya* [Encyclopedia of Palestinian terms and concepts]. N.p.: Palestinian Center for Regional Studies.

Ismail, Salwa. 2007. "Islamism, Re-Islamization and the Fashioning of Muslim Selves: Refiguring the Public Sphere." *Muslim World Journal of Human Rights* 4 (1). https://doi.org/10.2202/1554-4419.1116.

Iwais, Mazen, and Emanuel Schaeublin. 2011. "Sacred Spaces and Funds: Awqaf Properties and Zakat Committees in Jerusalem." In *Eternal Tour: Jerusalem*, edited by Donatella Bernardi and Noémie Etienne, 160–169. Geneva: Labor et Fides.

James, Erica Caple, ed. 2019a. *Governing Gifts: Faith, Charity and the Security State*. Albuquerque: University of New Mexico Press.

———. 2019b. "Policing Philanthropy and Criminalizing Charity in the 'War on Terror.'" In *Governing Gifts: Faith, Charity and the Security State*, edited by Erica James, 141–159. Albuquerque: University of New Mexico Press.

Keane, Webb. 2015. *Ethical Life: Its Natural and Social Histories*. Princeton, NJ: Princeton University Press.

Kelly, Tobias. 2006. "Documented Lives: Fear and the Uncertainties of Law during the Second Palestinian Intifada." *Journal of the Royal Anthropological Institute* 12 (1): 89–107.

Khalidi, Dima, et al. 2006. *Informal Justice: Rule of Law and Dispute Resolution in Palestine*. Birzeit: Birzeit University Institute of Law Report.

Khalidi, Raja, and Sobhi Samour. 2014. "Neoliberalism and the Contradictions of the Palestinian Authority's State-Building Programme." In *Decolonizing Palestinian Political Economy: De-development and Beyond*, edited by Mandy Turner and Omar Shweiki, 179–199. Basingstoke: Palgrave Macmillan.

Khalifeh, Sahar. (1976) 1999. *Al-Ṣabbār* [The cactus]. Beirut: Dar al-Adab.

Khatib, Ghassan al-. 2010. *Palestinian Politics and the Middle East Peace Process: Consensus and Competition in the Palestinian Negotiating Team*. London: Routledge.

Khayyat, Abdul-'Aziz al-. 1993. *Al-zakāh wa Taṭbīqāt-hā wa Istithmārāt-hā* [Zakat and its applications and profitable uses]. Amman: Ministry of Awqaf and Islamic Affairs.

Kocher, Victor. 2011. *Terrorlisten: Die Schwarzen Löcher des Völkerrechts* [Terror lists: The black holes of international law]. Vienna: Promedia.

Kochyut, Thierry. 2009. "God, Gifts, and Poor People: On Charity in Islam." *Social Compass* 56 (1): 98–116.

Koltès, Bernard-Marie. 1986. *Dans la Solitude des Champs de Coton*. Paris: Editions de Minuit.

Kuran, Timur. 2003. "Islamic Redistribution through Zakat: Historical Record and Modern Realities." In *Poverty and Charity in Middle Eastern Contexts*, edited by Michael Bonner, Mine Ener, and Amy Singer, 279–293. Albany: State University of New York Press.

Lacey, Robert, and Jonathan Benthall. 2014. *Gulf Charities and Islamic Philanthropy in the "Age of Terror" and Beyond*. Berlin: Gerlach.

Laidlaw, James. 2000. "A Free Gift Makes No Friends." *Journal of the Royal Anthropological Institute* 6 (4): 617–634.

———. 2014. *The Subject of Virtue: An Anthropology of Ethics and Freedom*. Cambridge: Cambridge University Press.
Leech, Philip. 2016. *The State of Palestine: A Critical Analysis*. London: Routledge.
Le Goff, Jacques. 1990. *Your Money, Your Life: Economy and Religion in the Middle Ages*. New York: Zone Books.
Lévi-Strauss, Claude. 1973. *Tristes Tropiques*. London: Jonathan Cape.
Levitt, Matthew. 2006. *Hamas: Politics, Charity, and Terrorism in the Service of Jihad*. New Haven, CT: Yale University Press.
Li, Darryl. 2020. *The Universal Enemy: Jihad, Empire, and the Challenge of Solidarity*. Stanford, CA: Stanford University Press.
Lundblad, Lars Gunnar. 2008. "Islamic Welfare, Discourse and Practice: The Institutionalization of Zakat in Palestine." In *Interpreting Welfare and Relief in the Middle East*, edited by Nefissa Naguib and Inger Marie Okkenhaug, 195–216. Leiden: Brill.
Maan News. 2010. "The Members of the Nablus Zakat Committee Hand In Their Resignation to the Minister of Awqaf." Accessed January 1, 2019. www.maannews.net/arb/ViewDetails.aspx?ID=319142.
MacIntyre, Alasdair. (1981) 2007. *After Virtue*. Notre Dame, IN: University of Notre Dame Press.
Mahmood, Saba. 2001. "Feminist Theory, Embodiment, and the Docile Agent: Some Reflections on the Egyptian Islamic Revival." *Cultural Anthropology* 16 (2): 202–236.
———. 2005. *Politics of Piety: The Islamist Revival and the Feminist Subject*. Princeton, NJ: Princeton University Press.
Malka, Haim. 2007. "Hamas: Resistance and Transformation of Palestinian Society." In *Understanding Islamic Charities*, edited by Jon B. Alterman and Karin von Hippel, 98–126. Washington, DC: Center for Strategic and International Studies Press.
Mauss, Marcel. (1925) 2016. *The Gift*. Expanded ed. Chicago: HAU Books.
Meari, Lena. 2014. "Sumud: A Palestinian Philosophy of Confrontation in Colonial Prisons." *South Atlantic Quarterly* 113 (3): 547–578.
Meneley, Anne. 1996. *Tournaments of Value: Sociability and Hierarchy in a Yemeni Town*. Toronto: University of Toronto Press.
Messick, Brinkley. 1993. *The Calligraphic State: Textual Domination and History in a Muslim Society*. Berkeley: University of California Press.
———. 2001. "Indexing the Self: Intent and Expression in Islamic Legal Acts." *Islamic Law and Society* 8 (2): 151–178.
Milton-Edwards, Beverley. 1996. *Islamic Politics in Palestine*. London: I. B. Tauris.
———. 2017. "Securitizing Charity: The Case of Palestinian Zakat Committees." *Global Change, Peace & Security* 29 (2): 161–177.

Mittermaier, Amira. 2013. "Trading with God: Islam, Calculation, Excess." In *A Companion to the Anthropology of Religion*, edited by Janice Boddy and Michael Lambek, 274–293. Oxford: John Wiley and Sons.

———. 2014. "Beyond Compassion: Islamic Voluntarism in Egypt." *American Ethnologist* 41 (3): 518–531.

———. 2019. *Giving to God: Islamic Charity in Revolutionary Times*. Berkeley: University of California Press.

Moumtaz, Nada. 2015. "Refiguring Islam." In *A Companion to the Anthropology of the Middle East*, edited by Soraya Altorki, 125–150. Chichester: John Wiley and Sons.

———. 2021. *God's Property: Islam, Charity, and the Modern State*. Oakland: University of California Press.

Nablus Zakat Committee. 1998. *The Nablus Zakat Committee, Palestine*. Booklet. N.p.: Nablus Zakat Committee.

———. 2001. *Al-Muyassir fī Aḥkām al-Zakāh* [Guidebook on the prescriptions on zakat]. Nablus: Nablus Zakat Committee, Section of Sharia Research and Studies.

———. [2000–2004?]. *The Nablus Zakat Committee, Palestine*. N.p.: Palestinian National Authority, Ministry of Awqaf and Religious Affairs, Zakat Fund Directorate.

Nashif, Esmail. 2008. *Palestinian Political Prisoners: Identity and Community*. London: Routledge.

Natsheh, Basel, and Cédric Parizot. 2016. "From Chocolate Bars to Motor Cars: Separation and Goods Trafficking between Israel and the West Bank (2007–2010)." In *Israelis and Palestinians in the Shadows of the Wall: Spaces of Separation and Occupation*, edited by Stéphanie Abdallah Latte and Cédric Parizot, 109–128. London: Routledge.

Nawawī, Abū Zakariyyā Yaḥiyā ibn Sharaf al-. (1200s) 1975. *Gardens of the Righteous*. London: Curzon.

Osella, Filippo, and Caroline Osella. 2009. "Muslim Entrepreneurs in Public Life between India and the Gulf: Making Good and Doing Good." *Journal of the Royal Anthropological Institute* 15 (1): 202–221.

Palestinian Authority Ministry of Awqaf. 2008. "Record of Transfer [of All Properties of the Pre-2007 Nablus Zakat Committee to the Palestinian Authority]." Signed on June 2, 2008.

PCBS (Palestinian Central Bureau of Statistics). 2015. *Labour Force Survey (July–September 2014)*. Ramallah: PCBS. https://www.pcbs.gov.ps/portals/_pcbs/PressRelease/Press_En_LFS-Q3_2014-e.pdf.

Pelham, Nicolas. 2014. "The Role of the Tunnel Economy in Redeveloping Gaza." In *Decolonizing Palestinian Political Economy: De-development and Beyond*, edited by Mandy Turner and Omar Shweiki, 200–219. Basingstoke: Palgrave Macmillan.

Perdigon, Sylvain. 2015. "'For Us It Is Otherwise': Three Sketches on Making Poverty Sensible in the Palestinian Refugee Camps of Lebanon." *Current Anthropology* 56 (S11): 88–96.

Petersen, Marie Juul. 2014. *For Humanity or for the Umma? Aid and Islam in Transnational Muslim NGOs*. London: Hurst.

Pierret, Thomas, and Kjetil Selvik. 2009. "Limits of 'Authoritarian Upgrading' in Syria: Private Welfare, Islamic Charities, and the Rise of the Zayd Movement." *International Journal of Middle East Studies* 41 (4): 595–614.

Qaddumi, Marwan Ali. 2012. "The Drinking Provision and Waqf Fountains in the City of Nablus (Al-Saqāya wa-l-Asbila al-Waqfiyya fī Madīnat Nāblus)." In *Conference on Manifestations of the Movement of History in the City of Nablus (Muʾtamar Tajalliyāt Ḥarakat al-Tarīkh fī Madīnat Nāblus)*. Nablus: Najah University.

Qaradawi, Yusuf al-. 2006. *Fiqh al-Zakat: Dirāsa Muqārina li-Aḥkāmi-ha wa-Falsafati-ha fī Ḍawʾ al-Qurʾān wa al-Sunna*. Vols. 1–2. Cairo: Maktabat al-Wahba.

Qutb, Sayyid. 2000. *Social Justice in Islam*. Translated by John B. Hardie. Oneonta, NY: Islamic Publications International.

Rahman, Tariq. 2022. "Landscapes of *Rizq*: Mediating Worldly and Otherworldly in Lahore's Speculative Real Estate Market." *Economic Anthropology* 9 (2): 297–308.

Ramallah Zakat Committee. 1997. *Leaflet Describing the Committee's Activities*. Ramallah: Ramallah Zakat Committee.

Rasanayagam, Johan. 2018. "Anthropology in Conversation with an Islamic Tradition: Emmanuel Levinas and the Practice of Critique." *Journal of the Royal Anthropological Institute* 24 (1): 90–106.

Raya News Agency. 2013. "The New Central Zakat Committee of Nablus Takes on the Tasks of Its Work." February 12, 2013. https://www.raya.ps/news/818541.html.

Rech, Walter. 2017. "Everything Belongs to God." In *Legalism: Property and Ownership*, edited by Georgy Kantor, Tom Lambert, and Hannah Skoda, 149–174. Oxford: Oxford University Press.

Retsikas, Konstantinos. 2014. "Reconceptualising Zakat in Indonesia: Worship, Philanthropy and Rights." *Indonesia and the Malay World* 42 (124): 337–357.

Reuters. 2018. "Thomson Reuters Unit to Be Renamed Refinitiv after Blackstone Deal." July 27, 2018. https://www.reuters.com/article/us-thomsonreuters-m-a-blackstone-group-idUSKBN1KH15H.

Rosen, Lawrence. 1984. *Bargaining for Reality: The Construction of Social Relations in a Muslim Community*. Chicago: University of Chicago Press.

Roy, Sara. 1995. *The Gaza Strip: The Political Economy of De-development*. Washington, DC: Institute for Palestine Studies.

———. 2000. "The Transformation of Islamic NGOs in Palestine." *Middle East Report 214* 30 (1): 24–26.

———. 2007. *Failing Peace: Gaza and the Palestinian-Israeli Conflict.* London: Pluto.

———. 2011. *Hamas and Civil Society in Gaza.* Princeton, NJ: Princeton University Press.

Ruel, Malcolm. 1992. "Christians as Believers." In *Religious Organization and Religious Experience,* edited by John David, 9–31. London: Academic Press.

Ryan, Caitlin. 2015. "Everyday Resilience as Resistance: Palestinian Women Practicing Sumud." *International Political Sociology* 9 (4): 299–315.

Salih, Tayeb. (1953) 1970. "Nakhla ʿalā al-Jadwal" [A date palm by the stream]. In *Dawmat Wadd Ḥāmid: Sabiʿ Qisas* [The doum tree of Wad Hamid: Seven short stories]. Beirut: Dār al-ʿAwda.

Samara, Adel. 2000. "Globalization, the Palestinian Economy, and the 'Peace Process.'" *Social Justice* 27 (4): 117–131.

Sana'a Center for Strategic Studies. 2020. "Tax and Rule: Houthis Move to Institutionalize Hashemite Elite with 'One-Fifth' Levy." October 6, 2020. https://sanaacenter.org/publications/analysis/11628.

Schaeublin, Emanuel. 2009. "Role and Governance of Islamic Charitable Institutions: The West Bank Zakat Committees (1977–2009) in the Local Context." CCDP Working Paper, Graduate Institute of International and Development Studies, Geneva.

———. 2009a. "Dawr al-Muʾassasāt al-Islāmiyya al-Khayriyya wa Uslūb Idārati-hā: Lijān al-zakāh fī al-Ḍaffa al-Gharbiyya (1977–2009) fī al-Siyyāq al-Maḥallī." CCDP Working Paper, Graduate Institute of International and Development Studies, Geneva. (Arabic translation of Schaeublin 2009)

———. 2012. "Role and Governance of Islamic Charitable Institutions: Gaza Zakat Organizations (1973–2011) in the Local Context." CCDP Working Paper, Graduate Institute of International and Development Studies, Geneva.

———. 2012a. "Dawr al-Muʾassasāt al-Islāmiyya al-Khayriyya wa Uslūb Idārati-hā: Muʾassasāt al-Zakāh fī Ghazza (1973–2011) fī al-Siyyāq al-Maḥallī." CCDP Working Paper, Graduate Institute of International and Development Studies, Geneva. (Arabic translation of Schaeublin 2012)

———. 2014. "Zakat Practice in the Islamic Tradition and Its Recent History in the Context of Palestine." In *Histories of Humanitarian Action in the Middle East and North Africa (HPG Working Paper),* edited by Eleanor Davey and Eva Svoboda, 19–26. London: Overseas Development Institute.

———. 2019. "Islam in Face-to-Face Interaction: Direct Zakat Giving in Nablus (Palestine)." *Contemporary Levant* 4 (2): 122–140.

———. 2020. "Disconnected Accountabilities: Institutionalizing Islamic Giving in Nablus (Palestine)." *Journal of Muslim Philanthropy & Civil Society* 4 (2): 28–60.

———. 2021. "Counting Good and Bad Deeds under Military Rule: Islam and Divine Bookkeeping in Nablus (Palestine)." In *Rules and Ethics: Perspectives from History and Anthropology*, edited by Morgan Clarke and Emily Corran. Manchester: Manchester University Press.

Schielke, Samuli. 2015. *Egypt in the Future Tense: Hope, Frustration, and Ambivalence before and after 2011*. Bloomington: Indiana University Press.

———. 2018. "Secular Powers and Heretic Undercurrents in a God-Fearing Part of the World." Keynote speech presented at the Secularity and Nonreligion Research Network Conference, King's College, July 5, 2018. https://allegralaboratory.net/wp-content/uploads/2018/11/KEYNOTE_Schielke-2018.pdf.

———. 2019. "The Power of God: Four Proposals for an Anthropological Engagement." *ZMO Programmatic Texts* 13:1–20.

Scott, James. 1987. "Resistance without Protest and without Organization: Peasant Opposition to the Islamic Zakat and the Christian Tithe." *Comparative Studies in Society and History* 29 (3): 417–452.

Sevea, Teren. 2020. *Miracles and Material Life: Rice, Ore, Traps and Guns in Islamic Malaya*. Cambridge: Cambridge University Press.

Shryock, Andrew. 1995. "Popular Genealogical Nationalism: History Writing and Identity among the Balga Tribes of Jordan." *Comparative Studies in Society and History* 37 (2): 325–357.

———. 1997. *Nationalism and the Genealogical Imagination: Oral History and Textual Authority in Tribal Jordan*. Berkeley: University of California Press.

———. 2012. "Breaking Hospitality Apart: Bad Hosts, Bad Guests, and the Problem of Sovereignty." *Journal of the Royal Anthropological Institute* 18 (1): 20–33.

Singer, Amy. 2008. *Charity in Islamic Societies*. Cambridge: Cambridge University Press.

———. 2012. *Constructing Ottoman Beneficence: An Imperial Soup Kitchen in Jerusalem*. Stanford, CA: Stanford University Press.

———. 2018. "The Politics of Philanthropy." *Journal of Muslim Philanthropy & Civil Society* 2 (1): 2–20.

Spadola, Emilio. 2011. "Forgive Me Friend: Mohammed and Ibrahim." *Anthropological Quarterly* 84 (3): 737–756.

Sroor, Musa. 2012. "The Role of the Islamic Pious Foundations [*Waqf*] in Building the Old City of Jerusalem during the Islamic Periods [637–1917]." In *Nuts & Bolts of Construction History*, edited by Robert Carvais et al., 2:229–236. Paris: Picard.

Stillman, Norman. 2017. "Charity and Social Service in Medieval Islam." In *The Development of Islamic Ritual*, edited by Gerald Hawting, 211–221. London: Routledge.

Taghdisi-Rad, Sahar. 2014. "The Economic Strategies of Occupation: Confining Development and Buying-Off Peace." In *Decolonizing Palestinian Political Economy: De-development and Beyond*, edited by Mandy Turner and Omar Shweiki, 13–31. Basingstoke: Palgrave Macmillan.
Tamimi, Azzam. 2007. *Hamas: Unwritten Chapters*. London: Hurst.
Tartir, Alaa. 2019. "Securitizing Peace: The EU's Aiding and Abetting Authoritarianism." In *Palestine and the Rule of Power*, edited by Alaa Tartir and Timothy Seidel, 227–247. Basingstoke: Palgrave Macmillan.
Tawil Souri, Helga. 2017. "Surveillance Sublime." *Jerusalem Quarterly* 68: 56–65.
Tripp, Charles. 2006. *Islam and the Moral Economy: The Challenge of Capitalism*. Cambridge: Cambridge University Press.
Tugal, Cihan. 2013. "Contesting Benevolence: Market Orientations among Muslim Aid Providers in Egypt." *Qualitative Sociology* 36 (2): 141–159.
Turner, Mandy. 2014. "The Political Economy of Western Aid in the Occupied Palestinian Territory since 1993." In *Decolonizing Palestinian Political Economy: De-development and Beyond*, edited by Mandy Turner and Omar Shweiki, 32–52. Basingstoke: Palgrave Macmillan.
Turner, Mandy, and Omar Shweiki, eds. 2014. *Decolonizing Palestinian Political Economy: De-development and Beyond*. Basingstoke: Palgrave Macmillan.
United Nations. 2009. *Human Rights in Palestine and Other Occupied Arab Territories: Report of the United Nations Fact-Finding Mission on the Gaza Conflict*. United Nations General Assembly: Human Rights Council. September 25, 2009. https://www2.ohchr.org/english/bodies/hrcouncil/docs/12session/A-HRC-12-48.pdf.
Volinz, Lior. 2018. "From Above and Below: Surveillance, Religion, and Claim-Making at Jerusalem's Temple Mount/Haram al-Sharif." *Surveillance & Society* 16 (4): 446–458.
Vom Bruck, Gabriele. 1997. "A House Turned Inside Out: Inhabiting Space in a Yemeni City." *Journal of Material Culture* 2 (2): 139–172.
Weber, Max. (1905) 2012. *The Protestant Ethic and the Spirit of Capitalism*. Mineola, NY: Dover.
———. 1946. *Essays in Sociology*. Oxford: Oxford University Press.
———. 2004. "Politics as a Vocation." In *Max Weber: The Vocation Lectures*, edited by David Owen and Tracy Strong. Indianapolis: Hackett.
Weizman, Eyal. 2006. "Walking through Walls: Soldiers as Architects in the Israeli-Palestinian Conflict." *Radical Philosophy* 136 (2): 8–22.
Werbner, Pnina. 1990. "Economic Rationality and Hierarchical Gift Economies: Value and Ranking among British Pakistanis." *Man* 25 (2): 266–285.
White, Hayden. 1980. "The Value of Narrativity in the Representation of Reality." *Critical Inquiry* 7 (1): 5–27.

Wikileaks. 2008. "Terrorism Finance: GOI Says Now Is the Time to Act against the Central Bank of Iran and Increases Its Financial Isolation of Gaza. Meeting on 29 July 2008 at the US Embassy in Tel Aviv." Accessed January 1, 2019. https://wikileaks.org/plusd/cables/08TELAVIV1742_a.html.

World Bank. 2015. *Economic Monitoring Report to the Ad Hoc Liaison Committee [on the Palestinian Economy]*. September 30, 2015. https://www-wds.worldbank.org/external/default/WDSContentServer/WDSP/IB/2015/09/29/090224b0 8310e894/2_0/Rendered/PDF/mainoreport.pdf.

Yahiya, Abbad. 2013. *Ramallah al-Shaqrā'* [Blonde Ramallah]. Ramallah: Dar al-Fil.

Zalzberg, Ofer. 2019. "Beyond Liberal Peacemaking: Lessons from Israeli-Palestinian Diplomatic Peacemaking." *Review of Middle East Studies* 53 (1): 46–53.

INDEX

Abu-Lughod, Lila: on honor of the weak, 62–63
abundance: aesthetic of, 37, 118; of divine generosity, 7–8, 99–103
accountability: and divine bookkeeping in dealing with zakat funds, 128; double bind under military rule, 51–52; and foreign intelligence services, 49; in interactions, 3, 64; through local reputation, 42, 52–57, 57–58
Afghanistan, 49
aid: to conceal signs of need, 61; counterterrorism targeting, 22; international, 17, 126–127, 130; mutual, 40; political control through, 128; zakat committees, 41–58
ajnabī. See whitey
ajr. See divine account
alcohol, 33–34, 28, 106, 135
anthropological vocation, 27
Arab Gulf: and Palestinian class formation, 123; as source of zakat donations, 17, 130; working in, 7
Arabic: of Israeli interrogators, 129; translating research into, 23

Arab revolutions of 2011, 21, 130; revolution in Egypt, 131; Tunisian Revolution, 73–74
Arab Spring. *See* Arab revolutions of 2011
Arafat, Yassir, 14, 18; governing zakat committees, 45
Arendt, Hannah, 130
Asad, Talal, 4, 24, 89
authoritarianism, 46; and Arab revolutions, 130; of the Palestinian Authority, 128; staying away from, 56–57
autonomy, 31, 33; competitions challenging, 98; ethical, 67; families, appearance of, 75; gift, rejecting as a sign of, 62, 64, 92, 95–98; of zakat committees, 44–45
'ayb (shameful): in interactions between affluent and destitute, 60–61; interlocutors, avoidance of roping into shameful interactions, 76; in market transactions, 92, 95–98; shamefulness associated with need, 70, 82; and zakat, 2, 83. *See also* shame

backgammon, 59–60
begging, 60, 69, 90; abstaining from, 80–81, 90
Blonde Ramallah, 25
body: of deceased, 113–117; of deceased exemplar of piety, 119–121; in fieldwork, 22; God sustaining, 99; during hosting, 29; polluting, 106; purifying, 87
Bouazizi, Mohamed, 73

calculation: breaking calculation apart, 104; calculative logic, 7, 99; giving, calculative framings, 102–103; in tension with generosity, 108–111; in zakat practice, 85–88
capitalism, 7. *See also* market
care of the self. *See* technologies of the self
cart (*basṭa*), 62, 66, 69, 72, 93–94, 96–97, 119; and the Tunisian revolution, 73–74
choked (*makhnūq*), 67
Christian(s): greetings, 4; and Islamic greetings, 35; money in the Christian tradition, 105; in Nablus, 15; during Ramadan, 36; technology of the self among early, 11; zakat, 48
compulsion: to be generous, 103; to give, 11–12, 76, 92–93, 98
concealing: and exposing of need, 59–74; and research ethics, 38–39; and respectability, 33, 82; transfers of wealth, 79–80
corruption: measures against, 45; of the Palestinian Authority, 19, 51, 54, 57; zakat committees as alternative to, 128
counterterrorism, 19, 57; donations affected by, 50; Islamic aid flows and, 19–22
covered (materially taken care of), 11; "covered families," 61, 63; by God, 65; neighbors, 76
cultural exceptionalism, in the study of the Middle East, 4

debt, 66; and divine accounting, 101; paying back, 68–69; and stickers in the market, 109; and zakat, 6, 49
demeanor, 31, 36; as source of scandal, 82; of zakat committee members, 52
desire: for freedom, 130; sexual, 65
development, economic, 91, 112, 126
dignity: appearance, need, and, 58; in Arab revolutions, 130; preserving in recipients of zakat, 48, 51, 53, 77, 79, 90; retaining without money, 59–74, 80, 88
divine account, 30; credit in, 8; deducting points from, 76. *See also* recompense
divine bookkeeping: disciplining effects of, 107–108; divine account, gaining points in as technology of the self, 11–12, 86–87; God as Bookkeeper, 100–103; during Ramadan, 102; zakat practice and, 8–12, 77, 87
divine money: definition of zakat as, 77; sensitivity of handling, 128; symbolic value under political repression, 112; zakat as God's wealth, 83; zakat gaining the status of, 3
divine provision (*rizq*): café as a source of, 59; different meanings of, 99; disciplining effect of, 106–107; God as Provider, 66, 82, 91, 98–100; God's sustenance, 83; lack of, 99; in the markets, 69, 92–111; on sticker, 66, 100, 109; usury, in contrast to, 106; withdrawal of, 119, 122; zakat, 91

INDEX

dizziness: from fasting, 69; from lack of nutrition, 64, 67
dollar, 109–110
due diligence, 51
duty to give, 75–91. *See also* compulsion

economy: ethical problems in a political economy of occupation, 126–129; in Nablus during fieldwork, 60; political, 6, 12, 17, 111, 123; of reward versus of blessing, 103; as social category, 4–5
Egypt, 6, 130–131, 73
empirical social research, in the Islamic tradition, 39
ethics: anthropology of, 3–5; ethical life, 12, 21, 39, 113; ethical problems in political economy of occupation, 126–129; ethical questions, 3; financial need, 76; Islamic tradition and, 3–5; as social exchange, 5. *See also* research ethics
ethnography: ethnographic stance, 23; under military rule, 22–40. *See also* participant observation
European Union, 17
evil eye, 84
exemplar, 47, 53; in giving, 90; historical, 119–121; merchants, as exemplars of piety, 105
exposure: and concealment of need, 25, 59–74, 97, 111; of market dealings, 96; scandalizing (*faḍaḥ*), 61, 66, 75, 82; shaming through need, 76

Fanon, Frantz, 40
fasting, 67; as collective practice, 35–38; in divine account, 101–102; as worship, 5; of zakat committee members on regular days, 53–54
Fatah, 14, 16, 45–46, 58; charitable society (Nablus), 78; zakat committee, loyalists on, 53–54
fieldwork, 22–40. *See also* participant observation; research ethics
Franklin, Benjamin, 109, *110*
funeral, 32, 113–118

gender: segregation and positionality, 25
generosity, vii; bragging about, 80; God's, 1–11, 83, 99, 121; of merchants, 100, 107–109; during Ramadan, 85; tension between calculation and, 103–105
Ghazali, Abu Hamid al-, 43, 81
gift: depersonalizing, 33, 70, 79; "poison" in, 92; as sale, 97; subordination through, 32; wounding effect of, 2, 12, 76
Gift, The, 7–12, 76, 92; and the social contract, 131
God: anthropological perspectives on, 4; Christian references to in interactions, 4; invoking to mitigate shamefulness of material want, 70, 83; Islamic references to in social interactions and greetings, 1, 30–31, 34, 60, 63, 65, 83, 117; in market transactions, 92–111; names of, 28; obligation to, 85; as source of all wealth, 82–83; on stickers or posters, 64, 66–67, 70, *102*, *104*, 110, *110*; support of, 112; sustaining ability to give, 9; trading with, 11, 101–104; in zakat giving, 7–12
Goffman, Erving, 3–5, 54, 64, 77, 89
good deeds (*ḥasanāt*), 30, 36, 76, 100, 118; deducting, 101, 114

gossip: accountability through, 42, 131; disciplining through, 125; about merchants, 109; and reputation of parties to a transaction, 60; and reputation of zakat committees, 52; zakat recipients, protecting from, 79
gratitude, 3, 26, 83, 103
Greeks, 11

Hacking, Ian, 4, 89
Hamas, 14, 18, 58; martyr, role in funeral of, 114–116; in Nablus, 16; war in Gaza Strip and Israel, 37; and West Bank zakat committees, 45–50; zakat tax in Gaza Strip, 6
Hammouz Café, 59, 81
Hanbali, Abd al-Rahim al-, 47–48, 121–122, 125–126
Hanbali Mosque, 43
ḥaqq. See rightful share
ḥayā'. See modesty; shyness
heart: of poor households, 48; reciting of Quran, 29; winning mind and, 50; zakat, effect on, 86–87; zakat, giving to win over, 6
hell, 103, 86, 128
Hereafter, 8, *102*, 128; passage into, 118; zakat, saving humans in the, 86–87. See also Judgment Day
Hizbullah, 57
honor, 38, 65, 82; family, 25, 75; in market transactions, 92–111; not caring about, 73; piety overruling, 90; virtues, in balance with, 111; of the weak, 60–62; women channeling zakat to protect men's, 84; zakat committee members and violation of, 52–53
hosting, 29–31; funerals, 117–118
humanitarian system, 6 humanitarianism and zakat, 130

'ibāda. See worship
iḥtirām. See respect
(in)equality: moral equality before God, 11, 22, 73, 83; problem of, 8; in zakat transactions in Nablus, 88–91
informal justice: committees, 18; Islamic institutions in Nablus, 43
intelligence services, 25, 28, 42, 45, 129; monitoring zakat expenditures, 51
interactions: ethnographic participation in *muʿāmalāt*, 26; ethnographies of face-to-face interactions, 131; face-to-face interactions, 3, 76, 83; in the Islamic tradition (*muʿāmalāt*), 5, 23; market transactions, 92–111; in Nablus, 15; transformation of, 35; walking behind coffins as part of *muʿāmalāt*, 114
intrusion (*tadakhul*), in other people's conduct, 67
irony: and material want, 59–74; among workers, 66–69
iṣlāḥ. See informal justice
Islam: decentering debates on, 4; as ethical tradition in lived practice, 4; as societal discourse, 4. See also Islamic public culture; Islamic tradition
Islamic public culture, 92–111; lateral disciplining, 113; popular stories, 118–122
Islamic tradition: accumulation of wealth, 106; anthropology in conversation with, 39; discretion, 51; lateral disciplining, 40; plasticity of, 5, 58; poverty, 81; research ethics, 39

Jerusalem, 12, 79–80
Jordan, 12, 31, 44; defining legal framework for zakat committees in

West Bank, 43; movement of people between West Bank and, 129; Muslim Brotherhood in, 57
Judgment Day, 100, 105, 117; fears of, 86–87; and inequality, 88

Keane, Webb, 3, 54, 89
knowledge on households in need: as generated by social networks in Nablus, 78–79; as generated by zakat committees, 47–49

lady of the neighborhood (*sitt al-ḥāra*), pooling information on poor households, 78
Laidlaw, James: on depersonalizing gifts, 90; on ethnography, 23
lateral disciplining: affluent people, disciplining into giving, 61, 65–66, 67; and Christians during Ramadan, 36; comparative study of, 39–40; definition, 5, 21; economic power relations, 112–132; ethical work on the self and, 77; in ethnographic fieldwork, 27; extreme form of, 106; givers and receivers, 60; through greetings invoking God, 34; to pray, 105; responsibility to look after people in need and, 89; social interactions as mutual disciplining, 58; of zakat committee members, 42, 54
Lebanon, 57, 73, 98, 131

Mahmood, Saba, 5; on piety and deference, 63
market, 21; detecting signs of need, 77; logic of, 7; Ramadan effect on, 95; transactions, 92–111. *See also* calculation
Masri, Munib al-, 24, 123–126, *124*
mastūr. *See* covered

material support, to designated terrorist organizations, 50
Mauss, Marcel: on alms, 7–8; citing the Quran, 131; on compulsion to give, 11; on gifts, "poison" in, 92; on gifts, wounding effect of, 2, 76; on social categories, 4–5; on social contract, 131
merit: divine, 103; spiritual, 7–8, 117; transferring divine, 87
Mittermaier, Amira, 7–8, 65; on economy of recompense versus economy of blessing, 103
modesty, 2, 53–54, 110; in comparative perspective, 73–74; shyness (*ḥayā'*), pious display of, 62–65; zakat givers displaying, 83
Morocco, 90
mourning, 32, 38, 114
mu'āmalāt. *See* interactions
Muslim Brotherhood, 14, 57

occupation: ethnographic work under, 24–27; of Palestinian territories, 14–19; political economy of, 112–132
orphans: sponsorship programs for, 17, 44–48; zakat for, 6
Oslo Accord, 14
Ottoman Empire, 12, 43

Palestinian Authority, 14, 18, 23, 42–47, 123; authoritarianism of, 128; banks and, 122; corruption of, 51, 54; Israeli economic relations to, 126; salary payments of, 95; sheikh in, 86; zakat committees, governing, 56–58; zakat committees, overseeing, 53
Palestinian Authority's Ministry of Awqaf and Religious Affairs, 41, 45–47, 53

Palestinian Liberation Organization (PLO), 14, 126
Paris Protocol on Economic Relations, 126
participant observation, viii; ethical considerations, 24; ethnographic participation in Islamic practices, 26–27, 35
patience (*ṣabr*), 2, 29, 54, 64
philanthropy, 7, 123, 125
piety: in balance with honor, 111; in contrast to making a living, 93; displaying signs of, 58, 79, 111; helping families as cultivation of, 80; as individual practice, 67; losing, 81; of merchants, 100; Muslim, 2, 42, 66; not caring about, 73; overruling honor, 90; pious giving and receiving, 24, 57, 75–91; pious reputation, 38; under political repression, 112; in public interactions, 5, 54; rejection or shyness to accept support as sign of, 61, 64; sharing information in the market as sign of, 106; and social responsibility, 12, 89; tombs of pious persons, 119; in zakat committee members, 54. *See also* virtue
police: in cemetery, 116; European and North American aid controlling Palestinian, 128; praying in shop, 107; and selling spaces for people in need, 69–73; and the Tunisian Revolution, 74; on zakat committees, 46
political pluralism, 46
popular confidence (trust): for soup kitchens, 56; in zakat committees, 17, 19, 46, 53, 58; for zakat projects, 56–57
power: British, 119; disciplinary power of zakat givers, 80; economic power relations, 19, 112–132; God's, 90, 104, 118; interacting with the powerful, 62; non-Muslim, 112; of poor people, 60; relations in research, 24; state, 6; structures, 25; tyrannical, 56
prisoners: exchange of, 114; political, 37, 50
private security company, 51
prophet(s): 27, 100, 105; invoked in popular saying, 71; zakat committee members and the qualities of the Prophet, 53
prostitute's decisive deed, 103
Protestant sects, 126

Quran: memorization (centers), 17, 43, 45, 48; Radio Quran Nablus, 29, 56; recitation and care of the dead, 117; recitation and care of the self, 80; recitation during funeral hosting, 118; recitation to claim selling space, 71–72
Qutb, Sayyid, 6

Rabin, Yitzhak, 14
Ramadan, 35–38; and divine bookkeeping, 102; effect on market, 95; giving sadaqa and zakat during, 62, 79, 84–88; selling stickers during, 69–70
Ramallah, 12, 97; cheap commodities in, 72–73; Nablus, in relation to, 16–17; as seat of Palestinian Authority, 14
reason (*'aql*), 110; in zakat practice, 85–89
recompense, 8, 30, 70, 81–87, 100–101; and death, 113; in expressing condolences, 117; house of, 118

reliance on God (*tawakkul*), 27, 27, 35, 54, 64–65, 99; as decisive good deed, 103–104; meanings of, 104–105
religion: commitment to, 56; as social category, 4–5; study of Islam, 4
religious skeptic, 27
repression, 42; ethical lives under, 16, 21, 113; malleability of zakat practice in face of, 60; in Middle East, 129; symbolic value of zakat under, 112; zakat committees between local accountability and, 57–58
reputation, 31, 41, 42; families, visible need and, 61, 82; in market transactions, 96; protecting reputations and research ethics, 38; tainting, 60, 97; of wealthy people, 3; of zakat committee members, 47, 52–53
research ethics: anonymization in the Islamic tradition, 39; and feelings of shame around acts of giving, 76; guidelines, xi; under military rule, 22–40
respect, 22; definition in context of Nablus, 29; ethnographic participation and, 27; loss of respectability, 75; mutual, 70; self-, 64, 90–91; zakat committee members as respected persons, 47, 53
ribā. *See* usury
rightful share (*ḥaqq*), 8; and just pricing, 100; and position of people in need in the market, 69; right to visit neighbors, 30; self-, 64, 90–91; and sense of justice underlying Islamic acts of giving, 131; society in balance and giving of the, 89–91; zakat as, 84
rizq. *See* divine provision

sadaqa (supererogatory giving): before the Islamic revelation, 11; on behalf of dead people, 107–108, 117–118; categories of beneficiaries, 6; to fend off misfortune, 84–84; flowing, 87–88, 107–108; and merchants, 100; in relation to zakat, 1; *waqf* as a subcategory of, 44
Samaritan(s): 15; rabbi playing backgammon, 59; and sale of alcohol, 33–34
satara. *See* covered
Saudi Arabia, 6, 44, 51
secret services. *See* intelligence services
security databases, 51
security forces: interacting with poor people, 72; Palestinian Authority, 128; policing funerals, 115–116; profiting from occupation, 127; and zakat committees, 46
September 11 attacks, 18, 49
sexuality, 65
shame: of exposing need, 68, 75–91; of a giver, 80; between givers and receivers, 60, 81; zakat giving and, 2–3, 25. *See also* '*ayb*
shyness: as cultivation of piety in social interactions, 5; between debtor and creditor, 68; dignity and, 73–74; rejecting support as a sign of, 61, 62
sign(s): of faith and piety, 79; lack of income and possible moral wrongdoing, 127; of material need, 75–78, 96–97; merchant commitment to social obligations, 106; "no credit," 109–110; in rejecting a gift, 62, 64, 92, 95–98
soup kitchen, 17, 44, 56, 56n22; in Cairo, 65
South Africa, 51

spying, accusations of, 24–25; in fridges, 77
steadfastness, 18, 91; and debauchery, 25; zakat transactions and, 112
Stoics, 11, 95
Sufi: circles meeting around shrines, 119; healing, 75; soup kitchen, 65; *waqf* funding Sufi *khanqahs*, 44
surveillance, 18, 24, 39; databases and international, 56; during funeral, 116; God-like, 129

tact: between affluent and those without money, 60; in giving, 2; lack of, 79–80; in responding to subtle signs of need, 73, 82; in zakat and sadaqa practice, 74
tadakhul. *See* intrusion
tawakkul. *See* reliance on God
technologies of the self, 3; as agency, 63; definition, 11–12; ethical self-fashioning, 63; self-cultivation, 5; zakat as part of, 86, 129
terror: financing of, 50, 56; lists, 19, 51, 57; war on, 20
Thawri, Sufiyan al-, 119–120, *120*
triadic reciprocity: between giver, recipient, and God, 8; between seller, customer, and God, 98–104
trust. *See* popular confidence; accountability
Tunisia, 73–74, 130

under pressure (*madghūt*), 67
'urf. *See* informal justice
usury, 106, 109, 121–122

vetting procedures, 56; of recipients against terror lists, 51
virtue, 2; display of, 3; God sustaining the virtuous, 118–122; and moral equality of those without money, 73, 90; Muslim life in community with others, 129; reliance on God as, 35, 105; zakat as, 58; in zakat committee members, 42. *See also* piety

waqf, 43, 45; definition, 44; as source of income of Nablus Zakat Committee, 44
water, of the path (*mā' al-sabīl*), 87, 108
Weber, Max, 126, 129
Weil, Simone, vii
whitey (*ajnabī*), 24–25
World-Check, 51
worship: in contrast to interactions and transactions, 5, 100

Yaish, Adly, 23, 27, 47
Yemen, 65, 73, 130

zakat: affecting passage into Hereafter, 128; calculating what is owed as, 85–88; categories of beneficiaries in the Quran, 6; collection and distribution system," 47–49; definition, 1; dual character of, 5–7; giving as sign of piety, 79; giving directly, 58, 60, 75–91; and global political economy, 6–12; invoking God, 83; as a loan to God, 8, 9, 85–88; military projects, 49; as passing on rightful share of wealth, 8–11, *10*, 82–85, *84*; as purification, 2; reason and heart in giving, 86–87; in tax systems, 6; triad of, 7; *zakat al-fiṭr*, 85. *See also* zakat committees; zakat law
zakat committees: forced closures of, 18–19, 22, 42; Nablus Zakat Committee, 23, 41–58, 60; origin of, 17; as perceived security threat, 49–52
zakat law: Jordanian, 43–45, 49, 52; Palestinian, 45

Emanuel Schaeublin is an anthropologist of the Arabic-speaking Middle East and Europe with a focus on ethics, conflict, and knowledge politics. He is a senior researcher at ETH Zurich and advises film productions.

For Indiana University Press
Tony Brewer, Artist and Book Designer
Brian Carroll, Rights Manager
Gary Dunham, Acquisitions Editor and Director
Anna Francis, Assistant Acquisitions Editor
Brenna Hosman, Production Coordinator
Katie Huggins, Production Manager
Nancy Lightfoot, Project Editor and Manager
Dan Pyle, Online Publishing Manager
Pamela Rude, Senior Artist and Book Designer
Stephen Williams, Marketing and Publicity Manager